ON THE ROAD TO SANTIAGO

ON THE ROAD TO SANTIAGO

▼

Bob Tuggle

Writers Club Press
San Jose New York Lincoln Shanghai

On the Road To Santiago

Writers Club Press
an imprint of iUniverse.com, Inc.

For information address:
iUniverse.com, Inc.
620 North 48th Street, Suite 201
Lincoln, NE 68504-3467
www.iuniverse.com

ISBN: 0-595-13910-8

Printed in the United States of America

To Marie

INTRODUCTION

▼

"After the Ascension, St. James, the Apostle, left Palestine and journeyed to Galicia in Northern Spain. In 44 A. D., he returned home and was beheaded by Herrod, but his body was returned to Spain for burial. During the 8th and 9th centuries, he was said to have appeared at critical moments on the battlefield as the Christians fought the encroaching Moors. His fame spread as Santiago Matamore (St. James, Slayer of the Moors) until, in 813, his grave was rediscovered at what is now Santiago de Compostela. The pilgrimages began almost immediately, with people flocking in by the thousands from all across Europe. Magnificent churches sprang up in Santiago and all along the pilgrim routes. By the 11th century, Santiago was declared the third Holy City and some 2 million people were making the trek each year. Today, people are still walking the route, aiming to arrive on July 25th, the saint's festival day."

The above is quoted verbatim from Thomas Cook's, *"On the Road Around the South of France"*, but there is no scientific proof that St. James ever set foot on the Iberian

Peninsula. What I suspect may have happened is that some bishops in Galicia talked to the Pope and bemoaned the fact that their area was devoid of any reasons whatsoever which would encourage people to visit and thereby promote commerce.

The Pope surely assigned the problem to one of his many committees to aid in a solution. They probably came up with the very unlikely St. James legend. As a bonus the church declared that those who completed the pilgrimage to Santiago during a Holy Year, the year in which St. James Day falls on a Sunday, would have their sins completely forgiven.

In 1999 St. James Day fell on a Sunday. The church made an exception with the year 2000. That was designated a Jubilee Year and the same indulgences would be granted. Those who made the pilgrimage any other year would have their time in purgatory cut in half. And, for those who were infirm or elderly, if they just walked to Villafranca del Bierzo they would get the same consideration.

It was surely successful. People have been walking to Santiago ever since. I'm not sure what evidence supports the above claim of two million people making the trek every year. Considering the overall population of Europe at the time, that sounds like a figure which has been blown way out of proportion. For a long time the walk was not popular, but in the last few years it has regained a lot of its former prominence.

About 20 years ago the indulgences were even extended to those who complete the journey by bicycle. There is a definite class distinction among those who make the journey. Neither the walkers, nor the refuge managers, consider the bicyclists as genuine pilgrims.

I had always been enchanted with Spain. When I arrived in Germany with the Air Force in 1955, I began to plan my first visit. Early one morning in April 1956, after taking an overnight train from Paris, I arrived in San Sebastian. That was the first Spanish city I visited and since then it has continued to be one of my favorites. That visit was to become the first of several over the next 43 years.

I first became acquainted with the Way of St. James *(El Camino de Santiago)* in the early 1970's when I read James Michener's book *"Iberia"*, but I did not give any thought to walking El Camino until I neared retirement in 1997.

I then put it out of my mind again, until one day when a good friend, Bob Stake, and I were discussing Bill Bryce's book, *"A Walk in the Woods"*, which related a walking journey on the Appalachian Trail. I told Bob I didn't think I would be able to accomplish that, because it would require you to carry too much. You would need a tent, a stove, a lot of food and other provisions. The thought of bears and rattlesnakes really wasn't appealing either.

But I told him there was another walk which I had read about that interested me much more. I told him about the old pilgrim's path known as "The Way of St. James". That conversation began to rekindle my interest in the walk. I said if I were to make the journey it would not be for any spiritual reasons. I thought it would be a great adventure and I would be able to see a lot of the Spanish countryside and meet a lot of interesting people. When you travel alone, you are more inclined to talk to strangers and meet more people.

During the last 1000 years a tremendous infrastructure has been built to provide comfort for pilgrims walking to

Santiago. I thought if the distances were not too great between refuges, I probably could make it. It is difficult to find a lot of information about the walk. I wanted to know exactly what villages you passed through and how far it was between each of the places where you might be able to stay. I wanted some very detailed information. It didn't seem as if that information was readily available so I patched together a walking schedule based on what I could find, mostly from the many books which I had collected over the years about Spain.

There were some short stories which had been written by people who had completed the walk. That information was rather sketchy and did not provide much detail, but related some interesting experiences. The best source that I found was Nancy Frey's book *"Pilgrim Stories: On and Off the Road to Santiago"*. While working on her doctorate she spent several weeks as a volunteer at some of the refuges. That provided some good detail on a few selected places. Another good source proved to be the Internet. My daughter, Gina, was able to extract a couple of dozen articles about El Camino which had appeared in newspapers over the past few years.

My first schedule consisted of 36 days of walking with a rest day in Pamplona, Burgos and Leon, making a total trip of 39 days. The longest distance for any single day was 21.5 miles, even though I had no idea whether or not I could walk that many miles in one day. I was allowing myself a week after the walk to visit San Sebastian once again and to travel to Bayeux, France to visit the American Cemetery at Normandy.

After I read Nancy Frey's book and Paul Coehlo's book, *"The Pilgrimage; A Contemporary Quest for Ancient*

Wisdom", I wrote a brief review of each book on Amazon.com, which is a common thing to do if you wish to state your opinion of a book. Amazon provides that service and it allows you to find out what other readers have thought of a book, before you buy it. In my reviews I included my e-mail address.

A few weeks later I was contacted by Teun Van Rooyen of the Netherlands. He had read my review and said he was also planning to do the walk. He was going to begin on March 15, 2000. His walk was going to be a little longer than mine. He was taking 6 months off from work and was going to start from his home in the Netherlands and walk through France to Le Puy en Velay, one of the historic beginning points, making a total journey of 1800 miles.

Through e-mail we became electronic friends. He is 44 years old and is a veteran walker. He was able to give me some very good pointers. I was curious to know if he thought I could really do this, because I was going to be nearly 63 years old. That probably wasn't a very good question, because he had no idea what shape I was in physically. He felt that I probably could do it if I took enough time in advance to do a lot of walking with the backpack.

In Europe there are a number of organizations which call themselves the Society of Friends of the Way of St. James. He said that he went to one meeting in the Netherlands and it appeared as if a lot of the members were around my age.

I had never given much thought to walking long distances. As a matter of fact, I really wasn't crazy about walking any farther than I absolutely had to for any reason. A good friend of mine walks for exercise and pleasure and has, on numerous occasions, invited me to walk with him. Fortunately, there was always some reason why I just couldn't do it. I never walked just for exercise or fun. I had to have a goal. Now that I had a goal, walking took on a totally different meaning.

In January I began walking in my neighborhood without the backpack. I had measured off a distance of one mile and started with that. I was surprised to find I was in such bad shape that even walking a mile was disagreeable. That really made me have second thoughts about this whole thing, but then I looked at it as a challenge, and I thought I should really be able to do this. I convinced myself that it would probably be a healthy thing for me to do.

When I first brought up this subject with my wife, Marie, and said I just might possibly try to do this, she said, "At your age? You've got to be crazy!"

When my grandson, Mike, heard about it, he asked me, "Now just exactly when are you going to start on this suicide mission?"

So with encouragement like that from the family, how could I not succeed?

When I would talk to Marie about this and ask her opinion about something, she invariably replied, "I'm not having anything to do with this!"

She was not impressed when I told her that even Shirley MacLaine completed the walk in 1994. Her reply was, "Well, she's weird too."

But Marie slipped up one day and did give me a good suggestion, and after that she was slightly more supportive.

At first I thought this was going to be a simple thing. You would just take your best shoes, a few decent clothes, a toothbrush, and be on your way. After doing some walking in my street shoes, and having sore feet after only a couple of miles, I started looking for some books about walking long distances. I found plenty and then realized that it's not as simple as just putting one foot in front of the other and grinding out the miles. I also discovered that my old Levis just would not do. They were made of 100% cotton and I learned that cotton is absolutely the worst thing to wear because it retains moisture and doesn't "wick". I didn't even know that!

There are such things as the right kind of boots for long-distance walking, walking in snow, walking in the desert, etc. etc. There were also special socks for walking, along with scientifically designed sock liners made out of polypropylene in order to give them just the right "wicking" factor. Certain drinks are "diuretic", so stay away from them when you're walking. I was learning new terms every day. It became a chore just to choose the right type of sleeping bag, and required several visits to the sporting goods store because I couldn't make up my mind. Should I go with down or should I go with a synthetic fiber?

I bought a good pair of Timberland long-distance walking boots along with the proper sock liners and pure merino wool socks. I must admit that when I put them on, I felt compelled to start walking. The boots seemed to fit perfectly and my new cargo pants with all the extra pockets and the zip-off legs were just right for any kind of weather.

I believed that I was finally outfitted to do some serious walking.

I walked a lot and was really proud of myself when I was up to five miles. At this time I was not thinking much about the backpack. I continued walking and over the course of the summer I improved to the point where I could walk twenty miles which, for me, was a great accomplishment.

Getting there had not been easy. In the beginning, my feet, legs, knees, and hips hurt a lot. The strangest thing though, was that my left leg came around pretty quickly. The right one constantly gave me problems. After some long walks, I would soak my feet in warm water for about an hour, and then I would limp and hobble around the house for the rest of the day. During all of this walking I never developed blisters. I believe that was because I progressed with the distances rather slowly. I didn't go from five miles a day up to twenty right away.

In July I began to do some serious thinking about the backpack. I took Mike's old Boy Scout backpack, a good external frame pack, and tried it on. It seemed a little snug, but after letting out all the straps and making as many adjustments as possible, it fit pretty well.

Several months ago I began to make a list of all those things which I would need to take along. The list grew and grew, but all of those things seemed to be necessary. I loaded up the backpack with everything I thought I would need, and tried it on. I weighed the pack and it was well over 35 pounds. It seemed to be pretty heavy, but I thought I would get used to that.

In early August I used the Internet to find a suitable airline ticket for my journey. Nearly all of the American and United fares had stipulations regarding a maximum thirty-day stay. That would not fit with my plans so I tried Air France. They had an excellent fare and there was no thirty-day limit. I figured seven weeks would be sufficient.

I filled out all the required information on the screen and then I sat there for a couple of minutes reflecting upon whether I really wanted to do this or not, assuming that once I pressed that key, there was no turning back. I thought I had to do it, I had already told too many people I was going to! I thought maybe I could say I now had a problem with my back. I did have a severe back problem at one time, so that should be believable.

I put all those thoughts out of my mind. I was convinced I could do it! After all, it's not as if I'm going to try to climb Mt. Everest, or something like that. So I pressed the enter key, and a message appeared stating that my ticket would be sent out promptly. My reservation was for a departure date of October 13th with a return date of November 30th. The ticket arrived within five days.

I also bought my train ticket over the Internet. It was going to be necessary to take a train to southern France and to take a train back to Paris from Santiago. I purchased a Europass which would allow me to travel any six days over a period of two months. A day or two after I ordered the pass I received a telephone call confirming the order. My pass was delivered by air express within the next two days.

Now the business of getting in shape had to be taken seriously. No more walking without the backpack. I began to walk in the forest preserve at Waterfall Glen which is only about five minutes from my home. I thought it might look a little stupid, or at least strange, for an old man to be walking around the neighborhood carrying a backpack.

The forest preserve was a perfect place to walk with the backpack, but even there it looked a little strange to some other walkers, bicyclists and joggers. Quite a few of them would stop and talk to me to find out just exactly why I was walking with a backpack. Only one walker out of the dozen I spoke to had ever heard of the Way of St. James.

The first week I walked four miles per day. It was a little struggle, but it really wasn't that bad. The following week I started walking eight miles per day. I was aching all over again, from my hips down to my toes. Fortunately, or unfortunately, my back wasn't bothering me at all, so that excuse couldn't be used. I had been following some of the advice in the walking books. I walked slowly, a little less than two miles per hour when counting the rest periods. I would walk for about an hour and then rest for ten minutes.

It was about this time that I received, from Teun, a book which turned out to be just what I needed. He had found a German handbook which provided the details on every village and refuge between St. John Pied de Port and Santiago. It was exactly what I had been searching for. There were distance figures all along the way. The book provided information such as the cost to stay at the refuges, if any cost at all, and whether or not the refuges were open in winter. That was very important to me, because I knew some of them closed after September, but I couldn't find out which ones. When a refuge was closed, the handbook even told you who had the key, and where they lived so you could pick it up and stay overnight. In some villages the key was kept at the local bar. This book would help me be much better prepared.

I was pretty rusty at reading German, but with the help of my dictionary I was able to make out about 70 per cent of it. I asked my good friend, Manfred Pfeiffer, to help me with those fine points which I couldn't decipher.

For the next week, except for walking, I was totally absorbed by this book every day. I was updating and revising my schedule to take advantage of all this new information. I was using Michelin maps with a scale of 1/400,000, but there were many villages and small towns listed in the book which did not appear on my maps. I was even able to correct a couple of instances where I was missing the path altogether!

After my week of eight miles per day, I realized I had to get everything out of the backpack which was not really essential. I was beginning to be concerned about being able to get anywhere close to twenty-one miles in one day.

There were also some other considerations. In order to avoid the blazing heat on the dreaded *La Meseta* (the plain), I scheduled my walking for late October and November, but that also meant the days would be getting a lot shorter, and the weather in Galicia would be even more unpredictable.

At a speed of less than two miles per hour it would take me more than eleven hours to walk twenty-one miles. It would be pitch black at night and that would not be a good time to be walking. My small flashlight would not help much.

With the help of the handbook, and by eliminating the three rest days, I was able to rearrange my schedule to eliminate those days of more than eighteen miles, even though I would now have thirty-nine straight days of walking. Eliminating the rest days probably was not detrimental because I ended up with a couple of days which would be short distances, probably no more distance than you would casually cover just wandering around a big city like Pamplona.

When you are walking alone you do a lot of thinking. I was usually thinking of things which I could throw out of the pack. Other thoughts also came to mind. Twenty years ago no one had wheels on their suitcases. Today, nearly every new suitcase you see has wheels. What would be wrong with wheels on a backpack? Because I was going to be walking through four fairly large cities such as Pamplona, with a population exceeding 200,000, wheels just might come in handy.

I decided that you would need a little bigger wheel than those which are on most suitcases. Those are pretty small and might not hold up. In 1979, two of my daughters, Gina and Laura, went to Europe with me and we stayed a month. We had Eurail passes so we were going to have to schlep our luggage around from time to time. I bought each of us a luggage dolly. That worked pretty well for awhile, but one of the dollies lost a wheel after too many cobblestone streets. So, for the backpack, I wanted a little bigger wheel.

I began looking in all the stores for a suitable carrier which I could modify to accommodate the backpack. There didn't seem to be much available which would work well. Eventually I did find one, and the metal was the same color as the pack and it looked as if it would be a perfect fit.

I took it home and attached it to the backpack by shoving the handle and body of the carrier between the frame and the pack. It fit perfectly, but it was a little too heavy. The luggage carrier weighed five pounds, and at this point I was even concerned about five ounces.

I thought I could chop off all the unnecessary parts of the carrier and somehow affix it to the backpack. I took the whole thing over to our shop and explained to my partner Manfred what I wanted to do. He had some additional ideas and went to work on it.

We ended up chopping three pounds of metal off the carrier and affixing it to the backpack so it looked as if it came from the store that way. Some time later I was browsing around one of the sporting goods stores, and what did I see? Backpacks with wheels! They were internal frame packs and the wheels were like those fitted to luggage. Not nearly as sturdy as my wheels. I thought that those wheels would provide me with just the little extra insurance that I might need.

During my daily walks I continued to ask myself whether or not the wheels would be worth the two extra pounds. I decided I would wait for awhile to make a decision. If I could successfully do eighteen miles per day, two days in a row without extraordinary pain, then I would keep the wheels. If not, they would have to go in order to get the weight down.

I continued to walk during August with the full backpack, wheels attached. In early September I was up to twelve miles per day.

My aunt and uncle paid us a visit and I stopped walking for five days. When I went out again, and continued the twelve mile routine, I felt really fresh. My right hip usually bothered me for the first hour and then it would settle down. That day my hip didn't start acting up until the eighth mile. I really felt good about that and I thought I just might be able to do thirteen or fourteen miles that day. I eventually did fifteen, but that night my feet and hips were making me suffer! I went to bed very early because I was totally exhausted. I thought maybe I had overdone it a little. The next day, however, I felt really good. My legs were fine and I could have walked again, but I'm not sure how far.

The following week I walked on Tuesday and Wednesday, sixteen miles each day. That was after laying off for four days. After the first day of sixteen miles, I was feeling fine. The second day was a different story. Once again, everything hurt. I was not feeling well at all that evening. I went to bed at eight o'clock and later was up most of the night with a bad cough. While I had been walking the weather had been quite cool in the morning so I had a jacket on along with the long pants. Within a couple of hours it was sunny and warm. Off came the jacket and the legs of the pants. When I would rest, the wind would strike my back which was wet with sweat. I think that may have given me a cold. I guess I should have put the jacket on while I rested.

Each day I was beginning to get a lot more realistic about how far I could walk. This prompted me to continue studying my schedule and fine tuning it wherever I could. I had already eliminated the rest days in order to avoid days which were more than eighteen miles.

One area which concerned me considerably was the area between Molinaseca and Cebrero. I knew that was going to be difficult terrain. At this place you are climbing toward Puerto de Pedrafita, which, at 4000 feet, is the highest point along the route. It is a treacherous mountain pass which is surrounded by 6000 foot peaks. The weather can be very unpredictable. There would most likely be plenty of rain, and in the middle of November even snow was a possibility. I had scheduled three days of walking which were 17.4 miles, 18.3 miles and 16.8 miles. Sixteen miles would be a great distance to cover on a steep grade, especially if the weather turned cold and rainy. By making some of the days in the earlier part of the walk a little longer I was eventually able to considerably cut down the daily mileage in this part of the walk by making it five days instead of three. My total number of days walking continued to be thirty-nine.

Just two weeks prior to departure I began to study the backpack situation again. I inventoried all the things which I was taking and when it was all spread out on the floor it didn't look like a whole lot of stuff. I thought I could even go with a smaller pack, but that would mean giving up the wheels.

I looked over the smaller packs which were available, such as the day packs. The Kelty Zephyr pack caught my attention. It weighed only 2lbs 3ozs and had 2300 cubic inches of storage space.

I decided to give up the larger pack and sacrifice the wheels. By making this switch I eliminated five pounds. The Kelty pack was also much more compact and easier to handle. I thought this was a good decision, even though I would be carrying it all the way. My total weight, including two quarts of water and some snacks, would now be about twenty-five pounds.

I began to check the weather in my four major cities, Pamplona, Burgos, Leon and Santiago. The low temperatures were in the forties and the highs were in the seventies. There were mostly sunny days and just a little rain. That weather was very typical of what we were having at home.

THE JOURNEY BEGINS

On Wednesday, October 13th, it was cool and there had been a little rain in the morning. The rain stopped in the early afternoon and the weather cleared up, but it was still pretty cool after several days of beautiful warm autumn weather.

I took an Air France flight from Chicago to Paris. I left Chicago at 5:45 PM Wednesday and arrived in Paris at 8:30 AM on Thursday. The plane was not crowded and no one occupied the seat next to me. It was a very comfortable flight. I actually got some sleep which was unusual for me on an airplane. This was one of my best flights to Europe. I felt good when I got off the plane and that was probably due to the fact I got some sleep.

After arriving at Charles de Gaulle Airport I went to the baggage area and waited until my backpack finally arrived. Prior to checking my luggage I had taken off the sleeping bag and carried it on board with me in order to avoid its getting detached from the backpack and lost. I put the sleeping bag on the backpack and then hoisted the whole thing onto my back, an exercise which I would repeat many times during the next seven weeks.

I found the train station, which was downstairs from the terminal and took a local train into the city. The cost was $8.46. The ride into the city was not a great pleasure. There were the usual ugly apartment buildings, with laundry and satellite dishes hanging from the balconies.

I got off the RER train at the Chatelet metro station and bought a carnet of tickets (10). The train which would take me to the south of France is an early morning train so I planned to stay in Paris on Thursday night.

I had a reservation at Hotel de France at 102 Avenue Tour Maubourg, near Invalides. I had visited the hotel in April, but I had forgotten exactly how to get there. After getting off the metro at Ecole Militaire I wandered around for a few minutes before finally asking a delivery man for directions. About that time I was thinking those wheels would really be handy now.

I got to the hotel and settled into my room. It was very nice and modern with a great view of the golden dome of Invalides from the window. I made another reservation for Monday, November 29th because my return flight was scheduled for the following day.

It was now about noon, so I walked the few blocks over to Rue Cler and had an egg and cheese crepe while sitting at a bench on the sidewalk just a few steps away. I followed that up with a chocolate eclair from the next door bakery.

After an espresso I took the metro to Gare Montparnasse. Even though I had a Europass for the train I needed to get a reservation for a seat because I was taking the high speed TGV (Tren Gran Vitesse).

Gare Montparnasse is a very big station, but after a short while I located the area where they handle tickets and reservations. The reservations office was closed and there was a computer printed sign taped to the door. I interpreted the sign to mean "moved, closed for an undetermined time."

There were about twenty other teller windows so I thought I would get my reservation at one of them. Every one of them had a sign up stating "position closed." It was just after one o'clock so I thought maybe they all went to lunch at the same time, even though that seemed a little strange.

About a dozen customers were milling around in front of the windows. From time to time a worker would come by and go inside. A woman worker walked up to one of the windows and taped up the same computer printed sign which I had seen before. I looked at the sign a little closer and noticed that the word "movement" was followed by "sociau". A gentleman with a briefcase was standing nearby and I asked him if he spoke English. He did, and very well too. I asked him what was happening.

He said, "Those buggers have just gone on strike." He was very upset over the situation, and continued, "They are public servants, and my taxes are paying their salaries! They only work about thirty-two hours a week, so what can they be striking for?"

I told him I needed to get a seat reservation on the TGV to Bayonne tomorrow and I wondered if they would be open in the morning.

"Do you already have your ticket?" he asked.

"Yes, I do," I said.

"Then I would just get on the train. Just tell the conductor those buggers are on strike. Speak English to him and he'll just overlook it," he said.

I thanked him for his help. In the lobby of the station I picked up a train schedule for the southwestern part of France and started to head back to the hotel. When I walked outside, I saw a cafe across the street. It was a nice day and I had plenty of time to spare so I went in and sat at the bar and ordered a beer.

I was studying the train schedule when I noticed that the same man, with whom I had spoken earlier, was entering the bar. I waved to him and he came over and took the seat next to me.

His name was Christian V and he was headmaster of a private school with 1000 pupils in Les Sables-D'Olonne which was on the Atlantic coast, south of Nantes. He had been headmaster for seventeen years and before that he taught English. He had been in Paris on business and was catching the three o'clock train back home. He had never been to the United States, but he said he hoped to visit Oshkosh with some of his friends next year, for the air show, because they were all airplane fanatics. His oldest son was training to become an airline pilot. He was very fond of Americans. He said he could still remember, as a young boy, waving to American troops when they had convoys going through his home town of Nantes.

On the way back to the hotel my mind was on something else as I was riding the metro, and I passed my stop. I decided to go on to the Trocadero stop. I got off there and walked to the park which was across the Seine River from the Eiffel Tower. I sat in the park and updated my journal while enjoying the view and the weather. It was sunny and warm. I walked from Trocadero to the hotel. Many people were waiting to go to the top of the tower. I counted 160 at one entrance and there must have been more than that at the other entrance.

After taking a bath I went out again to Rue Cler and took a table in the Café du Marche. It was now a little after six o'clock and they did not start serving dinner until seven. I ordered a beer and sat there watching the people on the street while I waited. There were two sets of tables next to mine and eventually two American couples (they didn't know each other) sat down. One couple was from Seattle. We had a pleasant conversation about Europe, and France in particular, while we had dinner.

On the way back to the hotel, I stopped in at a small café and had my final espresso for the day. It was only nine o'clock, but after the flight I was now getting pretty tired. I went to bed right away, but I woke up at one o'clock wide awake. I got up and began to read one of the three Agatha Christie mystery novels which I had brought with me to pass the time. After a couple of hours, I was able to get back to sleep. I had left a wake up call for five-thirty and I told the desk clerk it was very important because I had to catch the train at seven-twenty.

At six o'clock I was walking down Avenue de la Tourville to the metro. It was very quiet at that time of the morning. The weather was cool and it was still dark. When I reached the station I went directly to the ticket windows. They were now open.

It must have been a short strike because the tellers were working again. I purchased my seat reservation on the TGV to Bayonne. The reservation cost $3.80. I had seat number 12 on first class coach number 12. Since there was still plenty of time before the train departed I went to one of the station cafes and had coffee and croissants.

The TGV is a great train. The seats are much more comfortable than airline seats and some have tables which you can use to do some work or spread out your newspaper and read. The ride is exceptionally smooth considering the fact you are travelling at speeds up to 185 miles per hour. The first stop was Bordeaux which is more than 400 miles from Paris. That distance was covered in three hours.

After Bordeaux the train slowed down and my arrival time in Bayonne was twelve o'clock noon. I needed to take a local train to St. Jean Pied de Port which is at the foot of the Pyrenees mountains on the French side of the border. The next train to St. Jean did not leave until three o'clock so I had some time to kill. It was a local train making all stops between Bayonne and St. Jean so no seat reservation was required.

I walked around Bayonne for a short while and had lunch at a sidewalk café. When I returned to the station I met two young men who were also going to St. Jean. One of them was Claudio, from Brazil, and the other was Matias, who was from Lausanne, Switzerland.

Matias had short brown hair and strange looking, bulging eyes. He was accompanied by his dog, Samba. Samba was six months old and he said he planned to take her on the walk to Santiago. I thought she was pretty young to walk such a long distance.

"I do expect some problems in Spain with Samba because the Spanish do not look at dogs the same way we do in Switzerland, or in France," he said. "In Spain, dogs are just beasts! I hope she will be able to make it. I'm planning on fifty days of walking."

Claudio, the Brazilian, was a lean, sturdy looking fellow, with strange symbols tattooed on both legs. He said he expected to take just twenty days for the entire journey, walking twenty-five miles per day.

I'm not sure how long it actually took him, but I think it must have taken more than twenty days. After the first day, I never did see him again.

When the train arrived all of us got on, including Samba. We were still in France and dogs are welcome on the trains. Matias and I sat across from each other and Samba lay under the seats.

It took about an hour to get to St. Jean. Six walkers and one bicyclist got off the train. We walked up the street together and found the office of the Society of St. James. There I was issued a pilgrim's pass. The gentleman who took care of that for me accompanied me down the street to the refuge at 55 Rue de la Citadelle. He took me inside and showed me where the bathroom and kitchen were and then showed me the room where I could stay overnight.

The room had five double bunks in it. Shortly, the three Frenchmen, Frederic, Vincent and Guillaume, who were also on the train from Bayonne, came into the refuge. They spoke about as much English as I did French, so we were not really able to communicate very well.

Frederic, who was short and thin spoke a few words of English. He was very friendly and we tried to talk to each other whenever we got the chance. He was a pleasant person.

Then Paco showed up. He was the bicyclist. He was from Spain, but he worked for Citibank and now lived in Miami. His wife was from Pennsylvania. He had worked for Arthur Andersen & Co. in Paris and London. Spanish, of course, was his native language, and he also spoke fluent English and French. He was in his early forties, had been married for twenty years, and had two teenage daughters. He met his wife when she was on vacation in Spain with her girlfriend, at which time Paco was a student at the university in Madrid.

That evening Paco and I had dinner together at Chez Dede. His command of French made it easy for me. We had duck and red wine. He told me he had borrowed the bicycle from his cousin who lived in Valencia. On the first day he was not going to take the route that was suggested for bicyclists. He said he was going to take the same route the walkers take because that is the old pilgrim's way. He planned to make it to Pamplona tomorrow, a distance of about fifty miles.

I did not see any women in the refuge and I was wondering if they had separate dormitory rooms for them. When we got back to the refuge that question was answered for me.

We found that we had another roommate, a young woman from Argentina. Her name was Alejandra Gabriella Castello, 33 years old. Alejandra was very pretty with brown eyes and long blonde hair. She was friendly and looked as if she was in great physical shape. She was wearing a wedding ring, but I never did hear anything about her husband, so I don't think she was married.

Alejandra had been a school teacher, but she was currently working for an Italian company in Germany. She said she could make a lot more money in Europe than in Argentina and when she had saved enough she was going back home and buy a house. She spoke Spanish, German and Italian, but very little English. My German, though limited, was much better than my Spanish so that's how we communicated.

While we were sitting on our beds talking that evening, the three Frenchmen decided to take inventory. They were getting worried, thinking they had too much weight. They asked me how much weight I was carrying and I said between twenty-five and thirty pounds.

They asked the lady who supervised the refuge if she would hold some stuff for them until they returned. She was a very friendly woman and she said she would be glad to do that. She brought a large laundry bag and they began to fill it. They had a three-cell flashlight with eight extra batteries, two blankets, extra shoes, and a number of other things. After finishing the walk and returning home they intended to drive back to St. Jean and pick up their belongings.

As I observed the other walkers in the refuge that night I realized nearly all of them were in their twenties or thirties. Once again doubts began to creep into my mind. I told myself it was too late for doubts and maybe it would just take me longer to get there than it did the younger people.

Tomorrow we would be walking to Roncesvalles. Although the village itself only consists of a few houses and the monastery and church, Roncesvalles is an important name in European history. It was here in 778 that Charlemagne's army was attacked by the Basques. Roland, one of Charlemagne's paladins, and his knights fought a rear guard action against the Basques to hold them off while the main forces of the army retreated through the pass. Roland and all his men were killed and the *Chanson de Roland* was sung by minstrels all over Europe in the middle ages recounting his bravery.

Charlemagne had gone into Spain to assist the Spanish in expelling the Moors and returning the country to the Christians. But while doing so, his army plundered and sacked Pamplona, which was the Basque capital. The Basques sought revenge and attempted to destroy Charlemagne's army. The last army to cross the pass was Napoleon's during the Peninsular War in 1808.

Day #1

▼

—St. Jean Pied De Port, France to Roncesvalles, Spain, 17 Miles

I did not sleep well. I'm not sure if it was due to the excitement of finally stepping off on the road to Santiago or the espresso I had after dinner. I probably slept for two hours. I got up at six-thirty and it was still dark. Everyone else started to get up too.

That morning I put my sleeping bag neatly on the floor and folded it up tightly in order to get it into the stuff sack. That would be the last time I did that so neatly. Thereafter, just like everyone else, I just grabbed the sleeping bag and stuffed it in the sack. Maybe that's why it's called a 'stuff sack'.

I was the first one to leave the refuge that morning. I started off at seven forty-five and after just a few yards on the dark street I saw a familiar dog running toward me. It was Samba. Matias was standing in the doorway to a hostel. He had stayed there overnight. The lady who owned the hostel warned him he would have trouble in Spain with Samba.

There was a small bakery just a few yards farther down the street. Through the window I could see a woman loading up boxes with pastries. I went inside and ordered a couple of croissants and coffee. While I was there I saw Alejandra and the three Frenchmen go past. I did not want to get too far behind everyone because I did not know what to expect on this first day, so I hurriedly finished my coffee, put on my backpack, and headed off.

Immediately outside the town, on the road toward the Pyrenees, there was a very steep hill. That hill quickly knocked the spunk out of you and you knew right away that this was going to be a day of serious walking. The backpack really felt heavy and I was gasping for breath before I got to the top of the first hill. And the only thing I saw when I got to the top, was a lot more hills. I was not used to hills at all!

The weather could not have been better. The air was refreshing and the sky was clear and bright blue. Although the sun was warm there was a constant breeze in the mountains. The view almost made the struggle worthwhile.

Matias and Samba passed me and for most of the day we were passing each other. We talked several times and I gave him a packet of my trail food. In addition to being a generous gesture, it lightened my load, and I was constantly thinking about that.

Eventually Paco caught up with me.

He said, "We've gone eight kilometers and I've pushed this bicycle six!" I thought we had walked further than that. Seemed like eight miles to me.

Paco said, "Bob, can you spare a little water? This bottle that I have does not hold much and I've already drunk nearly all of it."

I had bought a one-and-half liter bottle of water the night before and I gave him a drink. I had already given Matias a drink and now I was beginning to wonder if my water would hold out for the whole day.

About mid-morning, a burly man, probably in his forties, using two ski-like staffs, came up behind me. We stopped for a few minutes and talked. His name was Willi, and he was from Austria. He had been a chef on a cruise ship and had visited America several times. He had apparently saved his money, because now he owned a restaurant in Flachau, Austria. He said that his wife and her girlfriend were following him.

As I looked back I could see two women coming toward us. One was of medium height and had blonde hair and blue eyes. The other woman had brown hair and was a little taller and heavier. Willi introduced me to his wife, Brunhilde, the blonde lady, and her friend Christina, who owns a small *pension* with twenty-three rooms in Flachau.

Last year Willi and Brunhilde had walked from Leon to Santiago. This year they were walking from St. Jean to Burgos and next year they intended to cover that stretch of camino from Burgos to Leon and then they would have completed the whole course. This was the first year that Christina had joined them. They always stayed in hostels and avoided the refuges. They were very nice people and I would see them off and on for the next several days.

Later that morning, I came across a young man sitting on the side of the road, with his boots off, rubbing his feet. He was just a bit taller than I, wore glasses, and had dark black hair, which was cut short. I thought that he wouldn't have a problem with this long walk because he looked very physically fit. He was carrying a big pack which looked quite heavy.

We made our introductions. His name was George. He was a chemical engineer, 33 years old, from Sao Paolo, Brazil. He offered me a piece of a chorizo sandwich and we sat and talked for a while. I then continued on my way.

About noon I had reached the highest point of that day's walk and was sitting on a rock taking a rest when George came by. He put down his backpack and then immediately snapped it back up and said, "Oh! Damn it!"

I said, "Yeah, you have to watch where you put your backpack. Those sheep have done their business on every square inch of this ground."

We walked on together for a short distance and I said, "George, you don't have to walk with me. If you want to walk faster just go on. I'm not a fast walker."

"I don't walk that fast either, and right now I've got a problem with my right foot. My big finger is really hurting," he said.

"I think you mean your big toe."

"Oh yeah, my big toe".

I found out later that George had dropped his canteen, which was full of water, on his big toe and smashed it pretty good. It was already turning various colors.

The day was sunny and warm. Walking up the steep hills carrying the backpacks was very strenuous and we were sweating a lot. We were also drinking a lot of water. George was out of water and mine was very low.

George had bought one of the Spanish guide books for the camino. It was an excellent book with all the maps and information needed to do a good job of planning your schedule. I wished that I had that book when I was making up my schedule.

"According to this map, there's supposed to be a fountain up here someplace," George said.

We met a young Spaniard walking toward us.

"Hello!" George said, "Is there a water fountain up this way?"

"Yes, there is," the young man replied, "It's only about five minutes ahead."

We walked for about another half hour.

"What the hell was he talking about! There's no fountain up here!" I said.

"You can't believe anything they tell you," said George.

A few minutes later we were walking on a path which was in a fairly deep depression. From the dirt wall there were two small pipes extending out about two feet and they were spewing water.

"Sir Bob, do you think this is the fountain?" George asked.

"It doesn't look like a fountain to me." I said.

Another Spaniard and his girl friend came by. They were not walking closely together and it was quite obvious that they were having a quarrel.

"Do you know if this water is drinkable?" George asked.

The young man was not interested in our problems right now. "I don't know," he answered, and continued on his way, walking away from the girl.

George and I discussed the water situation and finally decided to pass it up. We were afraid it was not drinkable and that we might get sick. About half an hour later we met two more Spaniards who were hiking to St. Jean.

"Do you know if there's a fountain up here?" George asked.

"There's no fountain, but a little farther up the way there's a cow trough and a hose," one of them said. "That water's okay to drink. It's about another half hour up the road."

We were now getting awfully thirsty and I said, "George, let's split the water which I have. We don't know if we're going to find that water or not."

At first George resisted taking any of my water, but after insisting, he and I finished whatever water was left. We were just hoping we would run across the cow trough and that the water there was good.

We eventually did come across the trough and there was a small hose running into it. We were so thirsty now that we really didn't care much whether it was drinkable or not. We filled up our water bottles and took some big drinks. It tasted okay.

We were now walking on a path which was loaded with rocks. At least the steep hills seemed to be behind us. But the rocks were terrible. After a while the bottoms of our feet began to hurt and there was nowhere we could walk to avoid the rocks. Paco must have had a hell of a time getting over these rocks with that bicycle.

We eventually came across a small road crew and asked them how far it was to Roncesvalles.

"It's only about a kilometer," one of the men told us.

"That doesn't sound too bad, George. We should be able to see it pretty soon," I said.

We walked for another hour and then came to the forest, which seemed to be principally beech trees.

"What does he mean, another kilometer, we've already walked at least two," George said. "I'm telling you, Sir Bob, they don't know distances!"

We would find out later, after looking at George's map more carefully, that there are two ways to get to Roncesvalles, and we had chosen the longest and most difficult.

We were now deep into the forest and we were trying to watch for the yellow arrows carefully, but in the dim light they were sometimes hard to see. It was also necessary to constantly watch where you were stepping because we were going down some steep slopes and the leaves covered small branches which would begin to roll when you stepped on them. The whole ground was covered with leaves and it was hard to determine whether or not you were on the path.

Nightfall was just about upon us. I was beginning to feel glad that I had teamed up with George.

After walking for about fifteen minutes without seeing an arrow, I said, "George, I haven't seen an arrow for quite a while. Do you think we're still on the path?"

"Well, it looks like a path, but now it's all looking the same to me," he said.

"Why don't you stay here and I'll go ahead another hundred feet or so and see if I can spot an arrow," I said.

It was now dark so I had to use my flashlight to shine on the trees looking for an arrow. After spending several minutes searching, I yelled back to George, "I don't see any."

I was beginning to get a little anxious and I could feel my heart beating a little faster. Being lost in the forest all night would not be a good start for the journey.

He shouted to me, "I think we had better backtrack to where we saw the last one."

We walked back, trying to stay on the exact path we had followed to this point. After searching for a while, we finally found a tree with a yellow arrow painted on it, and both of us breathed a sigh of relief.

By now we had lost at least half an hour or more. We carefully followed that path and within a few minutes it was pitch dark. We were using our flashlights to look for yellow arrows and we were trying to watch the path at the same time. With the loose wood under the leaves, and small depressions in the ground, the walking was difficult and it would be easy to take a fall.

It seemed as if we had walked for a long time when George said, "There's a light over there!"

"Where? I don't see one."

"Over there! Through those trees," he said.

"Oh, okay, I see it, but George that's a hell of a long way off. Do you think that's where we have to go?" I asked.

"I really don't know," he replied.

We continued walking and finally we saw other lights which were considerably closer. We still had quite a way to go and the going was slow because we had to be very careful where we stepped.

Had it been necessary for us to spend the night in the forest, we would have come through it without much of a problem. It seemed to be a pretty friendly place. There were neither mosquitoes nor bugs, and in Spain the wildlife is practically non-existent. They've killed just about everything that can be eaten. For the next 500 miles we would only see one squirrel and two rabbits.

It was eight-forty-five when we finally walked into Roncesvalles, twelve and a half hours after leaving St. Jean. That walk was only supposed to take eight hours according to our book. At that time we did not realize we had taken the long route.

The hospitalero and his wife signed us in and assigned each of us a bunk. Everyone else had already arrived. They told us they lock the place up at ten o'clock and if we wanted anything to eat we should quickly go next door to the café and get something. By this time we were hungry.

When we walked into the café, I heard someone start singing, "Chicago, Chicago," imitating Frank Sinatra. It was the Frenchmen and Alejandra. Matias was also with them. The Austrians were at another table and they waved to us.

"Hey Bob, you made it!" said Matias. "We were wondering what had happened to you."

"Well, we got lost in the woods for a little while," I said.

Our dinner consisted of wine, a good noodle soup and then trout with french fries.

"I'm not really crazy about food when it's looking back at me," said George. The trout came with it's head and tail still attached.

We got back to the refuge a few minutes before ten o'clock. While George was arranging his things, I went to clean up before going to bed.

I had returned and was organizing my things for tomorrow when George came back from the washroom and asked me, "Sir Bob, did you see the toilet?"

"You mean the Turkish toilet?" I said.

It was the type of toilet which is still found all over France, and sometimes in Spain. There is a porcelain square on the floor, with a hole in it. At least they give you two imprints so you will know where to place your feet. I always thought they could have also put some handles on the walls so you could keep your balance.

"Is that what they call it?" George said.

"The one next to it is a western type toilet," I said.

"I know, but a woman keeps monopolizing it. She comes out for a few seconds and then she goes right back in again," George replied.

"Yeah, I saw her too," I said. "I think that maybe she's sick."

Before going to bed, I had been able to take a lukewarm shower which quickly turned cold. While I was getting ready for bed I was trying to decide what I could throw away. The weight of our backpacks, in addition to food, had been one of the main topics of discussion today. I threw out my knife and fork, even though they were just plastic and probably didn't weigh anything. I threw out my can opener and decided I just wouldn't buy anything to eat if it was in a can. I even threw out the soft inner soles of my shower shoes.

George was carrying a lot more things than he really needed. He had binoculars, a Walkman, tapes, a knife which could be used for multiple purposes, and a compass. He also had a snake venom extractor kit, even though there are only two types of poisonous snakes in

Spain and they are pretty rare. He was also carrying a small rock which he brought from Brazil to place by a major cross along the camino. I tried to talk him into throwing it away, but he said he just couldn't do that after carrying it all the way from Brazil.

Matias had run into his first of many problems. The manager would not let Samba stay in the refuge at Roncesvalles. Since Matias would not sleep inside without Samba they offered him the room downstairs where they stored the bicycles. He and Samba spent the night there and it worked out pretty well. At least they were inside. It probably wasn't much worse than where we were sleeping, because we didn't have any heat either.

That night I slept for only about three hours. Although my feet felt fine, my legs were aching so much from the knees to the ankles that it kept me awake.

Day #2

▼

—Roncesvalles to Zubiri, 14 Miles

I got up at six-thirty and looked outside. It was raining slightly. No one else was stirring. At this time of the year it doesn't get light until about eight o'clock.

I noticed they had staffs for sale in the refuge so both George and I bought one. That turned out to be a good investment.

I told George I would meet him at the café next door for breakfast. I thought it would be open early, but I had forgotten that they don't get going in Spain until at least eight o'clock and sometimes nine o'clock.

The café did not open until eight-thirty. George came over about ten minutes after eight and found me sitting on the bench outside. While we were sitting there we saw Alejandra and the Three Musketeers walking down the road to the pilgrim's path. They did not eat in the restaurants. They were conserving their money.

Several other people were milling around outside waiting for them to open. I met an older man and his wife from Canada who were riding a tandem bike. He had worked for a bank in Canada and was now retired. They were planning to make it to Pamplona today. It had quit raining and we hoped it would be another nice day.

We had gotten our coffee and bread, butter and marmalade and were beginning to sit down when I heard someone say, "Hey Bob, I'm glad to see you again." It was Paco.

Surprised, I said, "I thought you would be in Pamplona by now."

"Oh, hell no!! Taking that bike over the pilgrim's path was a big mistake," Paco replied. "I pushed it most of the way and when I got here last night I was so exhausted I couldn't go any farther."

He had breakfast with George and me and when we parted, I said, "Good luck. Now this time, I'm sure I won't see you again. You'll make it past Pamplona today."

After a short walk on the path we came to the village of Burguete, which was described in Hemingway's novel, *The Sun Also Rises.* There was one main street and the houses were similar to small fortresses with bars on the windows and everything was locked up tight. As we walked through the town, we saw only two or three people which isn't unusual in these small places.

In the sixties and seventies many of the young people went to Germany to work in the factories because there was high unemployment in Spain. Although Spain has made tremendous strides industrially in the last couple of decades, the majority of that growth has been in the large cities such as Bilbao, Barcelona and Madrid.

Tourism still ranks as one of the biggest growth businesses in the country, but it just cannot support many of these small villages. With the older people dying off, and no one coming in to take over these homes, the places are deserted.

From Burguete the path lead off into farmer's fields and through groups of small trees. The sky was still overcast and there were dark clouds approaching. Soon we began to see bright bolts of lightning streaking across the sky and hear tremendously loud claps of thunder. We quickly took off our backpacks and pulled out our ponchos. We had barely gotten them on when it started to rain heavily. It was a downpour and it rained off and on all that day.

It was not long before we were into the worst part of the walk today. The path was only about four feet wide and it sloped down from both sides toward the center. It was loaded with rocks and the rocks ran in veins, many with sharp edges. The walking was very slow because you had to calculate nearly every step and be careful because the rocks were also very slippery from the rain. It was raining so hard that water was soon running down the path and we were actually walking in a ditch.

"I know why my sins are going to be forgiven," said George. "I'm being punished now. My feet are killing me!!"

"Are your boots waterproof, George?" I asked.

"Yes sir, they are," he replied.

I said, "That's very important, because if your feet get wet it's easy to get blisters."

The Austrian army overtook us about one o'clock. We later caught up with them when they stopped for a snack.

We went into a little café and pulled off our ponchos and backpacks. We made quite a wet mess on the floor because it was still raining pretty hard and the ponchos shed a lot of water. I asked George if he would tell the lady who owned the café that we were sorry for making such a mess on her floor. She said it was okay, no problem.

We joined the Austrians at their table and had a sandwich and a hot chocolate. This was the second time that George and I had stopped. Maybe that's why our average mileage was pretty low.

For the rest of the day we walked through sharp rocks, mud, and heavy rain. I was glad I had bought the staff because it saved me from several falls that day.

As we were walking, George casually said, "Well, when I get home, I guess I'm going to have to talk to that man who sold me these boots!"

"Why?" I asked.

"I don't think that they are one hundred percent waterproof," he said.

There was no need to tell George to try to avoid the water. It was impossible.

It began to get dark and we were still some distance from Zubiri. Out came the flashlights again, but now walking in the dark was even more treacherous because of the sharp rocks. We knew we had to cross the Arga River by way of an ancient bridge to get into the village, but we could not find it. Eventually we found the bridge and followed the arrows to the refuge. Once again, it was after dark, and we were the last ones to arrive. I began to think we were really bad at this.

When we entered the refuge, Alejandra and the Musketeers were making their dinner of soup and sandwiches. They asked us if we wanted to join them. We thanked them but declined and said we would go to a restaurant. They said there was only one restaurant and it was a few hundred yards farther up the road.

We found a bunk and put our backpacks down. There were only a few empty beds left and I was forced to take an upper bunk, which I did not like because I knew I would have to get up in the middle of the night and go to the washroom. I hoped the person below was a pretty sound sleeper.

As we walked up the street, I told George, "I hope this isn't a real nice restaurant."

"Why not?", he said.

"George, just look at us. We've got about an inch of mud on our boots, and our pant legs are splattered with mud all the way up to the knees."

"You're right. We don't look very good, do we?" he said.

When we got to the restaurant we looked in the window before entering. We saw several other pilgrims eating dinner and it wasn't a fancy place at all. We went on in and took a table. We started with a hot bowl of soup which we really needed because we were cold from the rain.

The other people we knew waited until we had finished eating and they walked back to the refuge with us. The Canadian couple I had met that morning was in the group. They said they could not make it any farther because it was raining so hard they felt it was just too dangerous to be on the road.

When we got back to the refuge we discovered there were two washrooms, one for men and one for women. The men's washroom did not have hot water, but the women's washroom did. The woman who managed the

place said we could take a shower in the women's washroom and she would tell the women not to go in there.

There were a couple of small heaters in the sleeping area
and all of those who had wet feet had placed their boots
next to the heaters to dry them. George put his boots there
too. My boots were really holding up very well. They were
completely dry and I was thankful for that.

Once again, I did not sleep well. I got up about one-
thirty, climbed out of the top bunk as quietly as I could,
and went to the washroom where I could turn on the
light. I sat in there on a bench and brought my journal up
to date. I went back to bed about three o'clock, and as I
climbed up I noticed that the elderly man from Canada
had been the unlucky one to take the lower bunk.

Day #3

▼

—Zubiri to Pamplona, 13 Miles

At six o'clock I was already organizing my things for the day. Because we were getting in after dark every day George and I had agreed we would get an early start today. He got up at six-thirty and started to get ready. His boots were still not completely dry so he put newspapers in them. He made sure he had dry socks to wear.

We left at seven-thirty and it was still dark and foggy, but at least it was not raining. With our flashlights we found our way back to the ancient bridge and crossed over it to get back on the path. It was more of the same, rocks and mud and occasionally piles of cow manure. We had to walk with our flashlights for the first half hour. The path continued to lead through farm land, ditches, mud holes, and cow pastures. At times it was very difficult to get around the mud holes without sinking three or four inches into the mud and water.

Today we were walking to Pamplona, a city which owes a great deal of its modern day fame to Ernest Hemingway. Hemingway wrote about the town in his 1926 novel, *The Sun Also Rises*. Jake Barnes, the main character in the story, had travelled to Pamplona from Paris with some friends for the **Fiesta de San Fermin**. The main event of the festival, held in July, is the running of the bulls. Today Pamplona honors Hemingway with a monument near the bull ring.

After a short while we reached Larrasoana. This was an attractive village which we entered by crossing the small 14th century Gothic bridge known as "the bandit's bridge" because, in the middle ages, it was a favorite place to rob pilgrims. At the refuge they are proud to show you the page which Shirley MacLaine signed when she walked through here in 1994. There are a lot of fine old houses in the village, many of which were being renovated.

There was one café in the town. We had a pastry and coffee. We were the only customers in the tiny place. The teenage girl who was waiting on us was listening to rock music and really didn't seem to have much enthusiasm for her job. She probably did not see much of a future here and likely was dreaming about the day when she would go away to Barcelona.

When we got back on the path we could see the Austrians ahead of us. They had passed us early today. It was fairly reasonable to assume that Alejandra and the Musketeers had also passed by while we were having our coffee. It looks as if we will be the stragglers again today.

"Mister Bob, did you hear someone scream last night?" George asked.

"No, I didn't hear anything, why?" I said.

"Well, someone was having a nightmare, because I heard some fellow screaming, 'No! No! No!' It scared me for a minute." he said.

It must have been due to the fact that I was thirty years older than he was that made George feel he should address me formally. I didn't feel comfortable with that.

"George, you don't have to address me as 'mister' or 'sir'. Just call me 'Bob'", I said.

"Oh, no, I couldn't do that. I just wouldn't feel right about it," he replied.

I didn't mention it again.

At noon we stopped to rest. George sat down and pulled off his boots and as he put his hand in one of them he exclaimed, "Wet! Wet! Wet! Waterproof, my ass!" He had brought along a couple of pieces of newspaper so he took out the damp paper and replaced it.

It was late afternoon when we reached the suburbs of Pamplona which is the capital of the Basque province. We passed through two suburbs, Villava and Burlada, and both of them seemed to be strongholds of the Basque nationalists. There were a lot of anti-government messages written on the walls along with many posters showing Basque terrorists who were wanted by the Spanish police. It was not a very pleasant place to walk. There were no smiling faces here.

"I was supposed to fly into Pamplona from Madrid, when I came to Spain," said George. "But it didn't work out that way. I took a direct flight from Sao Paolo to Madrid and then I was supposed to take a plane from Madrid to Pamplona. After we left Madrid they made an announcement that the airport in Pamplona was fogged in and they were re-routing us to Vitoria. As you know,

Portuguese is my native language and I'm just learning Spanish. They said it so fast I didn't understand what they were saying. When we landed I thought we were in Pamplona, even though I thought Vitoria was a strange name for the Pamplona airport. I got my backpack and went out the door of the airport and asked a man where I could get the bus into Pamplona and he told me, with an astonished look, that there was no bus from there to Pamplona. I went back to the airline counter to inquire about it and the woman told me all the passengers who had been on the flight, at that very minute, were getting on a chartered bus which would take them to Pamplona. It was then that I realized I was in a different city."

"So how did you get from Pamplona to St. Jean?" I asked.

George continued with his story. "I took a bus from Pamplona to Roncesvalles and got my pilgrim's pass there and stayed overnight in the refuge. That was pretty nice because they had a special church service in the evening for the pilgrims. The next morning I took a taxi from there to St. Jean because I wanted to start walking from the proper place. And that's when I met you."

"Now I know why I didn't see you in the refuge at St. Jean the previous night," I said.

It looked as if we were going to finish before dark today and we were really feeling good about this little accomplishment. The refuge was in the center of the old part of town, next to the cathedral. There was an iron gate at the doorway and just behind that there was a small area to park bicycles. We saw the tandem bike. After ringing the bell several times, the door was finally opened. It was the Canadian couple. Once again they had decided to stop due to the rain.

I told the man, "I hope I didn't disturb you too much when I got up in the middle of the night."

"You didn't disturb me at all," he replied, "I have trouble sleeping so I took a sleeping pill and I didn't know a thing until the next morning."

Both of us groaned when they told us the refuge was on the fifth floor. Our legs were aching after the long walk so we made good use of the banisters to help pull ourselves up the five flights of stairs. When we got to the fifth floor we went to the reception area and signed in. We were surprised to learn that, other than the Canadians, we were the only ones there. We assumed Alejandra and the Frenchmen must have gone on to Cizur Menor which is only three more miles.

We selected our bunks and unpacked those items which we were going to need for the evening. I went through my things to see what I could throw out. I put my French phrase book and the three Agatha Christie novels on the window ledge and left them there in the event someone else might want to have them. I hated to get rid of the French book, because I was probably going to need it later, but I was getting desperate to shed weight.

After taking a shower I changed into my rain pants and blue long sleeved shirt, which were the only other clothes I had. While I was in the washroom I noticed there was no toilet paper so I retrieved one of the mystery novels and tore out about 50 pages and put them in my backpack in the event they might be needed in the future. I thought at least these refuges could supply toilet paper.

Some restaurants provide a special price for pilgrims if you show them your pass. From the receptionist we got the name of one of those restaurants and went out to have our dinner. When we exited the building we ran into the Austrians in the plaza. They had checked into a hostel and were now going to the refuge to get their passes stamped.

It was about seven-thirty when we found the restaurant. We had wine, noodle soup, beefsteak, french fries and ice cream, all for $7.00. That was quite a bargain in Pamplona.

When we got back to the refuge I was surprised to see Alejandra, looking as if she were in pain and shuffling along in the dormitory.

I said, "I thought you had passed us while we had coffee in Larrasoana."

"Not today! Our boots were still a little wet this morning and after an hour or two of walking we were getting a lot of blisters. The longer we walked the worse our feet got. Toward the end we had to walk very slowly," she stated, as she pulled off one of her house slippers. I saw she had tape on three of her toes and a lot of tape on her heel.

"I have a lot of blisters on both of my feet, and so does Frederic and Guillaume. We just got here a little while ago. We are not going to make it very far tomorrow, probably only to Cizur Menor," she said.

"I've got some alcohol, band aids, scissors and a blister kit. If you want to borrow anything, just let me know."

"Oh yes," she said, "I think I would like to borrow some of that. Thank you very much."

DAY #4

▼

—PAMPLONA TO PUENTE DE LA REINA, 16.5 MILES

.

George and I left the refuge before eight o'clock and started finding our way out of Pamplona. It is a city of about 200,000 population so there was no problem finding a café for breakfast.

After we had a couple of cups of coffee we began following the yellow arrows through the outskirts of the city. We walked out through the University of Navarre campus and over the expressway toward Puente de la Reina.

During the Middle Ages it was an important city along the camino. There are two major pilgrim routes over the Pyrenees. The route which we had taken from St. John Pied de Port was the most common of the two. There is another way, known as the Aragon route, which crosses the Pyrenees at the Somport Pass. Puente de la Reina is the junction at which those two major pilgrim routes from France converge. The bridge, after which the town was named, was built over the Arga River around the 12th century to facilitate the passage of the pilgrims.

This whole day went pretty well. There was just a little rain and we only walked the wrong way for about fifteen minutes.

We had to go over a small mountain which was only about 2700 feet high. On the ridge at the top there were a dozen giant modern windmills producing electricity. Just before we got to the top the Austrian army passed us.

The rest of this day was uneventful. The path was not muddy, but loaded with rocks of all sizes. We got into Puente de la Reina before dark and settled down in the refuge.

George and I were sitting outside on a bench resting our aching feet when an American woman appeared and asked us where she could get her pass stamped. She introduced herself as Margaret, from San Francisco. She was the first American I had seen.

Margaret was of medium height, had very dark hair, and smooth skin. It was difficult to estimate her age, but I thought that she must be in her late forties. She wore glasses and was attractive. She was wearing blue jeans and a blue jacket and carried a small day pack.

That evening we had dinner at a nearby restaurant with Yarra Perez and Miguel Isanta. Yarra, 30, was from California, but she was born in Mexico and spoke Spanish fluently. She had been in Europe for a couple of years and had worked in France as well as Spain in the health care field. She specialized in helping people with learning disabilities. Her friend, Miguel, 45, was from Barcelona. We would see them both fairly regularly for the next few days.

Margaret was sitting at the next table. She came over and asked, "How high was that mountain we crossed today?"

She was referring to Sierra del Perdon, and I replied, "It was about 900 meters."

"I'm sure I saw it stated in kilometers," she said.

"No, that can't be right. It was only 900 meters and even if it had been more, it would not have been stated in kilometers," I said.

She then went back to her table. She heard George say he was from Brazil so she came back over to let us know that her son-in-law was from Brazil, but he now lived in San Francisco.

Day #5

▼

—Puente De La Reina to Estella, 12.5 Miles

I was awakened by thunder and lightning. It was raining and water was pouring off the roof of the refuge. I had bought a cheap wristwatch especially for this trip and by pressing a button on the watch the face of it would light up. That became a handy feature at times like this. I could see that it was just five-thirty and I was hoping the rain would let up a little before we left that morning.

We left the refuge at eight o'clock and there was now just a slight drizzle. We found our way to a nearby café for coffee. It was a smoke-filled place and a couple of people were already drinking beer. The only pastry they had were magdalenas, which are small individually wrapped muffins. They are pretty good and you find them in cafes all over Spain. We began to carry three or four of them in our backpacks for little snacks during the day.

After leaving the cafe we found our way to the Calle Mayor which lead us to the *Puente de los Peregrinos* (Pilgrims' Bridge). The bridge is of Romanesque construction and has six semi-circular arches. It has the typical hump-backed shape. It is a beautiful old bridge and has been well maintained.

Within a few minutes we were on the edge of town and walking into the countryside. As a result of the downpour during the night, the track was extremely muddy. Shortly we came to a shallow gorge with a steep descent of about fifty feet and then an ascent of about the same distance on the other side. George went down first and I could see it was very slippery. It was all mud and unfortunately there were no rocks to provide a firm step. As I descended I lost my footing about half way down and took a fall on my back against the side of the hill. I landed on my backpack and that broke my fall. I was jarred pretty good and, although I wasn't hurt at all, I thought I might be a little sore the next day. That did not turn out to be the case. Luckily there were no after affects at all.

During the day we met Monica and Christine, two Swiss Air stewardesses. They said that they often travelled to Spain to walk when they have a few days free. They were just walking for three days this time. We stopped at a café and had lunch with them. The cafe was owned by a middle aged couple. There was a dining room where the tables were covered with white cloths, nice napkins, glasses and silverware. There was another room by the bar which was more common with bare wooden tables and chairs near a wood-burning stove. We were not going to have a full meal so we elected to sit in the room by the bar. Although we were only having soup and bread the owners told us to take a table in the nicer dining room. We were a little muddy and wet so we insisted on taking one of the plain tables, but thanked them for their courtesy.

Just a few minutes after we left the cafe we met Margaret. We talked with her for a while and then she walked on ahead of us.

We arrived in Estella around five-thirty. The refuge was new and modern and very clean. We were asked to pull off our boots and leave them in the reception area.

After getting a bunk I went back to the lobby and retrieved my boots and took them outside where there was a sink and cleaned them off.

I saw Matias' signature in the registration book, but I heard that he was staying someplace else, because they would not let Samba in the refuge.

Estella was established in 1090 and became an important stopping point for pilgrims on the way to Santiago. It was the residence of the Kings of Navarre in the 11th century. It is a very attractive town with a population of 15,000, and the old part of the town is still a bustling shopping area.

George and I needed to do a little shopping so we walked to the old part of town. I needed to buy a new poncho because my cheap one had been ripped apart by the wind. I also needed spare flashlight batteries. The flashlight had become one of the most important things we carried.

We found a sporting goods store and I was able to buy a bright yellow poncho as well as batteries. George wanted to buy a pair of pants, but this store did not have any. We were given directions to another store. We found it a couple of blocks away. They did not have pants either. However, there was another store next to this one, but we only saw women inside.

George asked me, "Do you think that's just a woman's store?"

"I don't know, but there are only women in there," I said. "Why don't you go on in and ask. My legs are really aching, so I'm going to sit out here on the sidewalk."

In front of one of the stores, I found a little ledge which I could sit on and rest my legs while George went into the store.

"Can I buy something in here?" he asked a saleslady.

"Is it for your wife?" she asked.

"No, it's for me," he said.

"Well," she said hesitatingly, "I guess so."

George bought a pair of black pants which were similar to sweat pants, but a lot tighter. There was no zipper in the front and he always thought they were women's pants.

"That's okay. I'll just use them at night," he said.

When we left the store we ran into Margaret.

She said, "Come on, I want to buy you guys a beer."

We went to a nearby café and had a beer with her. She was staying at a hostel because no blankets are provided at this refuge and she does not have a sleeping bag. She did not want to buy one because it would add too much weight, and she didn't like the refuges very much any way.

After we left Margaret we went to find a place to have dinner. While we were eating, George asked, "Bob, do you think Margaret has had a face lift?"

I said, "Gee, I don't know. I didn't even think about that, but the skin on her face is pretty taut. I was thinking she was in her late forties, but now you're putting doubts in my mind."

"Did you notice her hands? he said. "They look much older."

On the way back to the refuge we stopped at a little store and I bought 2 peaches, 1 apple and a candy bar to eat on the trail tomorrow. I couldn't resist eating the candy bar that night.

DAY #6

▼

—ESTELLA TO LOS ARCOS, 13 MILES

We left the refuge before eight o'clock. It was cold early in the morning, but it got warmer after the sun broke through the clouds. This turned out to be a great day for walking. It was not raining and it was cool enough to keep you from sweating a lot.

George was a big fan of the American cinema. As we walked we discussed all kinds of films. He especially liked scary movies such as "Night of the Living Dead", "Dracula", "Psycho" and the television series, "X Files". He also liked a lot of American music. Whenever I would inquire as to the condition of his feet and legs, he would invariably reply, with his best James Brown imitation, "I feel good!"

When we weren't talking about movies, we were usually discussing another subject which was most dear to our hearts, and that was food. You could always depend on George to have some food in his backpack. He would carry apples, peaches, grapes, candy bars, magdalenas and on one occasion he had a couple of cans of Coca Cola. He didn't carry all of these at the same time because of the weight.

At times we would stop early in the morning at a café and buy a sandwich to take along for our lunch. Most of the time we would eat the sandwich a couple of hours later and then stop for lunch too. You do get pretty hungry when you are walking a lot. In this regard George and I made a great team. Neither of us ever hesitated to stop in at little cafes. Even though we ate a lot I could tell that I was beginning to lose some weight.

We had been walking for quite some time when we found a shady spot and some large rocks. The rocks made perfect chairs so we decided to take a rest.

Some distance away we saw a figure in a red jacket walking toward us at a pretty good pace. Even with George's binoculars we could not tell who it was. We thought it was probably Willi because the walker was using two staffs, but we didn't see Brunhilde or Christina.

After he got closer we did recognize that it was Willi. Even though we had rested for some time we thought we would wait until he arrived. Both George and I spoke some German and Willi spoke just a little English so our conversations with him were always a mixture of both languages.

"Hello guys!" Willi said as he approached.

"Hi Willi," we said.

"Where's Brunhilde and Christina?" I asked.

"They are coming, but I think they're pretty far back because Christina is having a problem with her leg today," he said.

"We thought you would be ahead of us by now," I said.

"We took the path which goes by the Irache Bodegas," Willi said.

"Oh, so you were doing some wine tasting," said George.

"So that's why we got so far ahead of you today," I said.

"Yeah, I think we stayed a little longer than we should have," he laughed.

George raised his binoculars up to his eyes and said, "I can see them in the distance now."

"Okay, Willi, we'll see you later. We had better get going if we want to get to Los Arcos before you do," I said.

We continued on our way. We were about 3 miles from Los Arcos and, with the advantage they had given us, this was the best chance we ever had of beating the Austrians. We walked and walked and kept looking for the town, but we couldn't see it. Eventually we turned a corner by a hill and Los Arcos was right there in front of us. Willi was only about a hundred yards behind. I'm sure he would have beaten us if he had not waited for Brunhilde and Christina.

The refuge in Los Arcos was relatively new and had forty beds, a kitchen and a dining room. The hospitalero was a Belgian volunteer. He told us there were days during the summer months when as many as 150 pilgrims arrived and he had no room for them. They had to sleep on the floor or outside in the large grassy area next to the refuge.

Margaret came by the refuge to find us. She said she was staying at the only hostel in the town and they had a restaurant on the second floor. George and I agreed to go over and have dinner with her that evening.

Although it was a small village, we had a hard time finding the hostel. It was very dark and there were few street lights. We finally located it and found Margaret having a drink in the café next door.

We sat with her until she finished her drink and then we went upstairs to the restaurant. As we were climbing the stairs it was obvious that Margaret was having problems with her feet.

The Austrians, who were also staying at the hostel, came in while we were eating and took a table. Brunhilde had her cell phone with her and she had not been there long before she got a call. In these modern times, even pilgrims can't get away from their business at home.

Margaret said she would like to walk with us tomorrow. She told us she had several blisters on one foot. She felt that if she had someone to walk with she might go a little slower and avoid more problems with her feet.

If she wanted to walk slower she was talking to the right team. I told her we might go only to Viana which was thirteen miles instead of trying to get all the way to Logrono which was nearly eighteen miles. I had jammed the nail on the little toe of my right foot and it was giving me a problem and George was still having trouble with his big toe. Other than that our feet were in good shape, and I didn't want to push our luck too much.

She said that going to Viana would be fine with her.

We suggested meeting her for coffee the next morning. The café across the street was part of the gas station and it opened at seven o'clock so we agreed to meet there shortly after it opened.

At dinner Margaret told us that she has a daughter in Amsterdam. She said her daughter, Jill, does free lance writing of promotional brochures and was now working on a project for Virgin Atlantic Airlines.

Margaret had taken a train from Amsterdam to Pamplona and started walking from there. George and I were teasing her saying, 'Oh yeah, all those sissies start in Pamplona so they don't have to fight those hills and rocks the first three days.' She said she was only going to walk to Burgos, which is about 100 miles away, and that Jill might meet her there and they would then travel in Spain for a few days.

When I asked Margaret how old Jill was, she responded, "I'm not telling you guys that! Then you'll be trying to figure out how old I am!" She continued to be very evasive when the subject of age came up.

Day #7

▼

—Los Arcos to Viana, 13 Miles

Again we woke up to rain and a blowing wind. I looked out the window at six o'clock and it did not look pleasant.

We met Margaret at the café a little after seven o'clock and had coffee and some pastries. It was still raining so I had an opportunity to try my new poncho. The poncho was the type which also covers your backpack. I was wearing my regular pants, rain pants, a tee-shirt, a long sleeved shirt, a jacket and my poncho.

I had only gone a couple of blocks when I realized that, although it was still raining, it was not cold enough to be wearing all those clothes. Before we got out of town I found a place to stop and George and Margaret helped me get out of the poncho so I could take my jacket off and put it in my backpack. The poncho, which was made out of a heavy plastic material, did not breathe. As you perspired the moisture gathered under the poncho.

We walked out of the town past the cemetery into the
farmland. Today we wished for a few rocks, but just a few,
because the path was pure mud and with the continuing
rain it was very slippery. You could not walk fast because
you were sliding in the mud with every step. After only a
couple of hours of this our legs were beginning to ache.
Before long our boots were covered with mud and were
getting very heavy.

George said, "With all this mud gathering on the bottoms of my boots, I'm getting taller every hour."

. A couple of days before, Margaret had picked up an old
tree branch and was using it for a staff. George exchanged
staffs with her and also loaned her one of his gloves.
George told her he would trim up her staff with his knife
and make it usable.

I was walking a few feet ahead and she was walking
with George and telling him all about California. I
thought that would be good for George. Margaret liked to
talk a lot and he could practice his English. She was also
talking about her daughter, Jill, in Amsterdam. She said
Jill had lived there for six years and was now speaking
Dutch fluently.

Before noon we were passed by Gennaro. Gennaro is
Italian and he did not speak any other language so we
never really got to know him. He carried the minimum of
everything and walked in open-toed sandals, with no
socks. The sandals did not have a good sole and we were
surprised that he was making such good time because he
was sliding all over the place in the mud.

George figured that Gennaro was walking the camino
as a penance and said he must have really done some bad
things to be punishing himself so much by walking in

those sandals. He was a fast walker and after he got a few hundred yards in front of us, Margaret just couldn't resist trying to walk faster too. She left George and after she passed me I told George I thought she was making a mistake trying to go too fast. I had told her there was no prize for the person who finished the quickest.

The Austrian army caught up with us about noon and we talked to them for a while. They said they were going to pass Viana and go on to Logrono. That would put them ahead of us by about a day, and that proved to be the last time we would see them.

It rained all day except for about an hour. After climbing one slippery hill after another we finally arrived in Viana with our boots caked with mud and our clothes soaked with sweat.

Viana is a very historic town, as all towns in Spain seem to be. The town was founded in 1219. It was here that Cesare Borgia, the evil son of the infamous Pope Alexander VI, and brother to Lucretia Borgia, was killed in 1507. He was originally buried in a tomb in front of the Church of Santa Maria, which was in the center of the old part of town. Cesare Borgia was such a wicked person that even two hundred years after his death his reputation still offended the clergy. Two centuries after he was buried here the Bishop of Calahorra ordered his tomb to be opened and for his bones to be taken away and buried under the road. There is still a marker in front of the church indicating he had once been buried there.

The refuge in Viana was a pretty nice one. Two young girls acted as receptionists and they were very helpful. I sat with one of them for awhile and practiced my Spanish. She told me the refuge in Navarette was closed and she gave me the phone number of "La Carioca" which is a hostel there.

Margaret had passed by the Viana refuge and had left us a note telling us she was going on to Logrono.

George said, "And with my staff and glove."

"I think she's overdoing it again," I said. Because she would now be a day ahead of us, there was a good chance we would not see Margaret again. Even though at times she could become a pain in the neck, both George and I felt bad about the possibility we might not see her again, because we had grown to like her a lot.

In the refuge there was a laundry room on the first floor with sinks where you could take off your boots and wash away the mud and do laundry by hand. We washed some of our clothes that night and draped them over the steam radiators in the room and the hallway. The radiators were hot and the clothes dried quickly.

After doing our laundry we went out to a local café and had a drink at the bar. The barmaid was about eighteen and we talked to her for a while. George asked her what she wanted to do in the future and she replied, with enthusiasm, "Oh, I'll probably be working at this bar the rest of my life."

George said to me, "Can you imagine that? She has no desire to do anything better in life than what she's doing right now."

George needed to replenish his newspaper supply for his boots. We located a small store and took care of that chore before finding a restaurant for dinner.

Most restaurants do not start serving dinner before eight-thirty or nine o'clock, but in some places you can find one which starts serving around eight o'clock. That was one of the things we were constantly asking at restaurants, because we liked to eat early. We also had to be aware of the time the refuge locked the doors. That time varied with every refuge, but it usually ranged between ten and eleven o'clock. If you were out after that hour they would not let you back in.

Day #8

▼

—Viana to Navarette, 14 Miles

The weather was perfect today, a little cool and no rain.

You could see Logrono from Viana. It was only about five miles away. Logrono is a big city and you have to walk across a long bridge over the Ebro River to get into town. George wanted to cash a travelers check so we walked into the center of town.

I found a place to sit and waited with our backpacks while George found a bank to handle his transaction. He came back after about half an hour and was telling me how difficult they had made it for him. He had not shaved for a couple of days and I guess he looked like a suspicious character so they wanted to take all precautions.

Just down the block from where I had been sitting we found a fifties-type cafe with chrome bar stools and two big horseshoe type counters. We had coffee and their special pastry which resembled a funnel cake.

We walked back toward the small street where we had seen the yellow arrows. We followed the arrows through the back streets, walked pass the refuge, and finally came to the edge of town.

As we passed a phone booth I suggested to George that maybe we should call the hostel in Navarette and reserve a room. We had no idea whether or not that was necessary, but it was probably the only place in town where rooms were available so we didn't want to take a chance. We decided we would get a double room and split the cost.

At the edge of Logrono there was a walkway which was about eight feet wide and it stretched about a mile out of town down the camino path. A lot of people were taking a stroll or riding their bicycles. The concrete path finally ended and we were in the country again.

This was our best day for walking and the path was the best so far, not too many hills, mud or rocks. We arrived in Navarette late in the afternoon and found the hostel on the main street.

George was curious about the name because "La Carioca" refers to someone who is a native of Rio de Janeiro. The hostel appeared to be a little run down but clean. No one was at the desk when we entered so we rang the bell which was sitting on the counter.

After a few minutes a man appeared and George informed him that we had a reservation. He asked for the name and George said, "Jorge."

The man said, "I don't have a reservation for a Jorge."

"I just called a few hours ago," George said.

"I have a reservation for a 'Jorge Miguel,'" said the man.

"Well, that's it! That's my name!" George said.

"You didn't say that!" the man said gruffly.

We got the key to our room, and lugged our backpacks up the stairs.

As we climbed the stairs, George said, "Can you believe that? He probably hasn't had anyone call for a reservation in weeks, and he's giving me a hard time about the name!"

I said, "He did seem to be a little hostile."

A few minutes later George went back downstairs to ask about something else and when he returned he said, "I think I know why he was upset. Apparently we interrupted their lunch. They are just now finishing eating."

We did not have to deal with that man again, which was fine with us. After that we always spoke to a woman, who was probably his wife, and she was very pleasant. She told George that a man who was from Rio de Janeiro had owned this hostel more than fifty years ago and that was the origin of the name.

I unpacked my little medicine bag, in which I was keeping those important things such as band aids, tape, scissors, Tylenol, Advil, alcohol and everything else which I thought I might need. My little toe was still causing me a problem. The nail had been jammed against the front of the boot a few times when walking down hill. I had started taping it up and that helped a little.

The arch of my right foot was also aching a lot. It had been hurting yesterday and this morning I put some paper under it to provide more support, but the paper shifted during the day and I think I did more damage than good. George gave me some cream, which was like BenGay, that he had bought at a local pharmacy. I massaged my foot for several minutes with it and that seemed to help.

We had dinner in the hostel dining room. Garlic soup is one of the specialties in this area and I decided to try it.

The main dish was roast pork with french fries, and we had ice cream for dessert.

The woman who owned the place prepared and served the dinner. The garlic soup was delicious and so was the roast pork. There were four other people in the dining room and I suspect that was everyone who was staying there.

Although the beds had clean sheets and the room was remarkably clean, both George and I used our sleeping bags that night. It just got to be a habit and we didn't have to worry about getting cold in the middle of the night. In some of these places they turn off the heat after midnight.

There was a very clean bathroom at each end of the hallway and one had a shower. Our room was not big, but the price was only $21, which we were splitting, so I guess you can't expect a suite for that.

Day #9

▼

—Navarette to Najera, 10 Miles

I woke up in the middle of the night and it was pouring rain. At seven o'clock the wind was blowing furiously. I looked out the window and some of the branches on the trees were bent down nearly to the ground. I told George we might as well sleep in this morning because the weather was atrocious and we only had ten miles to walk.

We left the hostel shortly after nine o'clock and went to the restaurant next door for coffee and toast. I bought two cockleshell pins for my cap, and I thought I would give them to my granddaughters when I got home, if I didn't lose them along the way.

The weather cleared up quickly and the sun came out. It was going to be a great day after all.

I had taped up my toes and heels as well as my right arch. I thought if there was any friction the very thin tape would protect my toes until I became aware that something was wrong. I was paying close attention to my right foot hoping the arch would not give me a lot of trouble that day. At any sign of trouble I always took off my boots and socks and checked it out. One day I suddenly became aware of a slight burning sensation in my right heel and after examining it I found a small wrinkle in the sock liner. That was the problem. After straightening it out every thing was fine. My socks and boots fit so tight I became aware of any little problem pretty quickly. I had now walked over one hundred miles without blisters and I was hoping to keep it that way.

We were living dangerously today. The path lead out of town via the main road. We had to walk a long way on highway N120. The N120 is a two-lane highway with a shoulder of about three or four feet.

We always walked facing the traffic, but we soon found in some cases that too was dangerous. When we came to the first curve which was a right hand curve for oncoming traffic we realized that many of the drivers cut the curve by taking a foot or two from the shoulder. After we discovered that, whenever we approached a right hand curve we would cross the road and walk with the traffic to our back until we passed the curve, then we would cross over again. This was time consuming and dangerous and it was not pleasant walking at all, especially with a lot of traffic, and all of it moving very fast.

As we were walking many of the drivers would honk their horns and wave to us. I said, "I think they are wishing us a good journey, George." With our backpacks and

staffs it was obvious we were pilgrims so that was a saluta-
tion which we heard very often.

"Or they may be yelling, 'You idiots!!'," he said.

After about five miles the path lead off the highway and
back into the fields again.

People walk the camino for various reasons. I was doing
it just for the adventure. I thought it would be a great experience and so far it had been more than I had expected.

Many people walk it for religious reasons. George said
he was doing it because he was at a crossroads in his life.
He said he had to make some big decisions so he wanted
to get away from everything and think.

He was educated as a chemical engineer and had
worked in a number of factories in Brazil. He spent five
years at a factory in the Amazon, living with snakes, spi-
ders and all kinds of other creatures. He specialized in
quality control in the manufacture of glass bottles. In
Brazil they make bottles for Anheuser-Busch, Gatorade,
Moet-Hennessey, Hellmann's and a lot of other familiar
names. He said they do everything possible to avoid man-
ufacturing glitches, but they happen from time to time.
He told me about the time they made a lot of bottles for
Anheuser-Busch and then discovered that the eagle was
facing the wrong way.

I asked, "How many bottles had you produced?"

"Three million," he replied.

George most recently had been working at a factory in
Sao Paulo and driving two hours each way getting to and
from work. He decided he either had to move closer to the
factory or quit. There was no decent neighborhood near
the factory so he decided to quit and that was why he had
time to go off and think.

He was involved with Sayonara, a 30 year old woman, who had a ten year old daughter by a previous marriage. She was a psychologist and George liked her and the daughter a lot. He was not so fond of Sayonara's mother, who was ultra-religious.

George said Sayonara's daughter did not want to study or read or learn anything new, she just wanted to play. George did not like that and the girl's mother could not see that there was anything wrong with it. He said he would like to have a child, but he would want the child to study and learn things. On top of all that, George's mother and father did not like his girl friend. Nevertheless, Sayonara was pressuring George to marry her and he was trying to make a decision about his future.

Another opportunity had come George's way, which he also had to consider. At one time he had worked for Owens-Illinois Glass in Brazil and his boss had been an American. George said that he was a tough ex-marine, and his motto was, 'Determine what has to be done, and then do it!'

Just a week before George left for Spain he received an e-mail from his ex-boss. He was working at a glass factory in India and he wanted George to come there and help him out for a few months.

George had a lot to think about.

As I mentioned above, dogs are treated differently in Spain than they are in France. In France dogs are welcome in restaurants, on buses, trains, and in taxis. That is definitely not so in Spain. Dogs are not considered nice house pets. They are used for the most part as watch dogs or sheep dogs. In Spain two of the biggest businesses must be security fences and watch dogs. Although you see all types of dogs such as rottweilers, dobermans, and mastiffs, by far the dog of choice is the German shepherd.

When walking through small towns the nice houses invariably are surrounded by security walls, usually constructed with bricks and concrete, and sometimes with broken glass cemented into the top just to discourage anyone who might want to climb over. In the front there would be a wrought iron fence with a strong security gate and two or three German shepherds, with their teeth bared, barking and straining to get at you through the gate.

Spain has a very low crime rate and the crime which they have is mostly petty theft, so I'm not sure why they feel compelled to live in these fortresses. When we walked into towns and villages we would usually see dogs. Fortunately for us, all the dogs we ran into which were not chained, were friendly.

In Paul Coelho's book he described his fight with a giant rottweiler in the abandoned village of Foncebadon. That was an allegory and the rottweiler represented his sins. Within the next couple of weeks we would have to walk through Foncebadon and George was always saying if he had to fight a wild dog there representing his sins, he hoped it would be a chihuahua.

Even though we walked slowly all day we arrived in Najera before the refuge opened at three o'clock. There was a café across the street and I told George I was going over there for a cup of coffee. He said he was going to sit there by the refuge and keep trimming his 'new staff' which he had inherited from Margaret.

The old man who ran the refuge was very cheerful. He was proud of the refuge and said that it was a 'five star' place, and it was pretty nice. He said they did not get many North Americans there. He said most of the Americans just drove on past.

Being the first ones there, we had our pick of the bunks. I took a shower while there was still hot water and then washed some clothes. We were on the second floor and they had clothes lines strung outside the windows.

This turned out to be a beautiful day with the sun shining brightly. The temperature was 65 degrees so I was sure my walking clothes would dry before morning. That was always something to take into consideration. The socks were heavy wool and if they did not dry I could always pin them to my backpack and they could dry as I walked, if it didn't rain. I had several pairs of socks so I never worried about not having dry ones on hand.

While we were sitting downstairs at the big dining table, David, a young Spaniard whom we had previously met, arrived and said, "I saw Margaret. She is on her way and should be here in about ten minutes."

"Well," George smiled and said, "at least I'll be able to get my glove back."

Since he had already started to keep track of our days of walking on the tree branch which he had gotten from Margaret I don't think he was concerned about getting his staff back.

We waited in the reception area and after a short while Margaret came in and, from the way she was walking, it was obvious immediately that she now had more serious problems with her feet.

She said that now both feet had a lot of blisters. She told me, "I should have listened, but I thought I could walk a little faster."

George said, "You're just trying to walk too far, too fast. You've got to slow down a little until your feet get accustomed to this."

Margaret was visibly aggravated with herself and replied, "I know! I know! I've learned my lesson now!"

"But where have you been?" I asked. "You should be a day ahead of us."

"I left you guys a note in Viana so you know I passed that place up, which turned out to be foolish, but anyway, I went on to Logrono, and when I got there my feet were in terrible shape. I couldn't even walk the next morning, so I had to stay over there an extra day. It didn't seem to help very much though."

That explained how we got back together again.

Margaret came upstairs with us and selected a bunk and then she asked, "Can you guys help me with my feet? I think I need to have the blisters burst and drained."

"I have a blister pack and some alcohol, but I probably wouldn't make a good doctor. Maybe George can do it," I said.

She pulled off her boots and socks and showed us her feet. With blood in one of the blisters, they looked pretty gruesome.

After George had taken a needle and sterilized it by heating it up he propped her feet up on his knee, and as I held the flashlight, he began to burst and drain each blister. She must have had eight or ten of them.

That evening some of our other old friends arrived. Alejandra, Vincent, Frederic, Guilliame and Matias with Samba showed up. They had been walking slowly and taking it easy on their feet and now their feet were beginning to heal.

Of course the hospitalero would not let Samba in the refuge so Matias had to look for someplace else to stay. Matias was sitting outside so I went out to talk to him.

He was mad. He said that even before he could ask any questions, the manager immediately said, 'No dogs!'

Later in the evening Alejandra told me someone had found a place for Matias and Samba to stay. I was glad to hear that because Matias told me they had to sleep outside last night.

It was quite a thrill seeing some of our friends again. It was here that we also met some new friends, Auxiliadora, Jacinto, Lourdes and Dominick.

Auxi and Jacinto were a young Spanish couple in their early twenties from Malaga. They were exceptionally nice and I liked them a lot right from the very beginning.

Lourdes and Dominick, also a young couple, were from the Basque province. Lourdes always introduced her boyfriend as Dominick because no one could pronounce his Basque name. The Basques like to use the 'x' and the 'z' as much as possible in their words making some of them practically unpronounceable.

Lourdes was shapely and attractive and seemed very confident. She wore glasses, was tall and had black curly hair and a pretty face. And she knew all this. But, she did not have a great sense of humor.

Margaret was fooling around and was pronouncing San Francisco with an accent and Lourdes couldn't resist correcting her. Thereafter, Margaret referred to Lourdes as 'the Spanish princess,' and, when leaving, she would always say '*hasta la vista*, baby', just because she knew Lourdes didn't like that.

George was learning Spanish and his grammar was far from perfect. Lourdes never missed an opportunity to correct him. When he referred to Najera as a *ciudad* (city), Lourdes said, "Najera is not a *ciudad*, it's a *pueblo* (village). Leon is a *ciudad*."

George muttered, but not in an angry way, "Damn! She just can't resist correcting me."

We were told that a medical helper who volunteers his time was coming by the refuge later in the evening. Margaret immediately put her name on the list. When he arrived he spent at least half an hour working on Margaret's feet. He did a real good job because she said they felt better after that.

I told Margaret I thought she should stay off the road for one or two days and give her feet a chance to heal. She would not hear of it. She insisted on walking with us tomorrow, but she said she would walk when I said 'walk' and she would stop when I said 'stop.'

After we had dinner we went back to the refuge and sat with the other pilgrims around the kitchen table and talked and took some photographs.

Some of the pilgrims were smoking. Guillaume always rolled his own cigarettes. Guillaume had long black hair down over his shoulders and a dark beard which had not grown in very well. I commented to Margaret about him being frugal and rolling his own cigarettes.

"Bob," she said, "do you really think that's tobacco he's putting in those cigarettes?"

"I thought so. But you're from San Francisco, so I guess you would know better than I if it's something else."

"Well, I'm not saying it's not tobacco, but I'm always suspicious when I see someone rolling their own cigarettes. He even looks suspicious to me."

"Oh, he's okay," I said. "I met him my first day in St. Jean. He doesn't speak any English so we really haven't gotten to know him very well, but I think he's okay."

There were a lot of people in the refuge that night. In the bunk next to me there was an Italian man who was older than I. He was over six feet tall and was very thin and wiry looking. He did not speak much English or Spanish, but I was able to understand that he had walked the camino several times. He had also walked from London to Rome, over 1000 miles, in 49 days. He said he was going to Belorado tomorrow, which was more than twenty six miles! He laughed when I told him we were only going to walk about thirteen miles. But then, he laughed after every statement and seemed to be a little crazy. I was glad when he finally turned his attention to some Spaniards who were occupying the bunks on the other side of him. They were amazed, and I heard one of them say 'he must just put his feet on automatic.'

Day #10

▼

—Najera to Santo Domingo De La Calzada, 13 Miles

The path was good today, fairly smooth and not too many hills. Again, the weather was perfect for walking. The sun was out, the sky was a bright blue, and there was a cool breeze.

Margaret's feet were still giving her a lot of trouble. She had just a small overnight pack for her necessities, no sleeping bag and boots that were more for fashion than hiking.

While walking behind her that day, I said, "Margaret, did you realize you are turning your left foot inwards all the time?"

She replied, "I know, I have to do that to keep it from hurting too much."

I finally asked, as politely as possible, "Did you give a lot of thought to this walk before you decided to do it?"

"What are you saying, Bob? Are you suggesting that I'm unprepared?"

"Well, it seems like that. You're wearing jeans, you have no sleeping bag, and those boots definitely are not for hiking. And you're not wearing the right kind of socks."

Margaret exclaimed, "Okay! Okay! So I'm not prepared, but there's a reason for it! Would you like to hear it, or do you just want to criticize me today?"

"Sure," I replied, "We want to hear it. Go ahead, tell us."

Margaret began to tell us the story about how she came to be walking the camino. About a year ago she was divorced after twenty years of marriage. We were later to find out it was her second divorce and that she had been married once before, for ten years. Sometime after the divorce she met a man working in a bookstore in San Francisco. He was an American who had been living in Australia for the past twenty-five years. His wife had died the year before and he decided to come back to America to see if he should move back permanently. He and Margaret began dating while he lived in San Francisco. They had even talked about marriage, but he then decided to go back to Australia. After he had returned home he decided he wanted to see Margaret again and he suggested that she come to Australia for a few months so they could determine if they were really meant for each other.

Margaret was working for a shipping company in San Francisco. Her boss was very moody and created a difficult atmosphere in which to work. At times he would go several weeks without even speaking to some of the people in the office. She decided that she was going to quit her job and go to Australia, but it was going to take her several weeks to make all the arrangements.

She had a condominium that she wanted to rent while she was gone and she had other matters to handle. She thought she should give the company at least four weeks notice, but her boss was being such a jerk that she decided to just give him two weeks notice. A day or two before she was going to give her notice he called her into his office. He told her the company was trying to cut expenses and her job was going to be eliminated. They would give her three months severance pay.

In order to get the most economical fare to Australia it was necessary to take a flight which made several stops. After two days she arrived in Melbourne. She found that her friend's house had been turned into a memorial to his deceased wife and two days later he told her that it just wasn't going to work. He said he knew it as soon as she got off the plane.

Margaret angrily said, "You would have thought the bastard could have told me that before I spent all that money and travelled two days to get there!"

Margaret called her daughters in San Francisco and Amsterdam. One of them said, "You've always talked about doing some meditation, so why don't you go to Thailand and do that?"

Being as she was already in that part of the world, Margaret thought that was a pretty sensible idea. She travelled to Thailand and Sri Lanka and spent about two months in a couple of monasteries meditating.

· After the meditation she went to Amsterdam to visit her daughter, Jill. Jill was very busy with her project and told her mother she couldn't get anything done with her around. She called her daughter in San Francisco and she suggested walking the camino because she had been talking about that.

So Margaret bought a pair of boots and a small pack and took off for Spain. The day she got off the train in Pamplona she started walking and that very same evening she met George and me in Puente de la Reina.

After this rather lengthy explanation, she said, "So Bob, you're right. I didn't have much time to prepare, but here I am anyway."

I said, "Well, at least one thing I can help you out with is sock liners. I have several and I'll give you one pair. They will help your feet by keeping them as dry as possible and if I were you I would get rid of those cotton socks whenever you get a chance and buy some wool ones."

As we continued walking, Margaret divulged a little more about her family that day. We discovered she had three daughters and a son, but we were still kept in the dark about their ages.

Santo Domingo is another important stop on the camino. It was founded in 1044 by St. Dominic the Hermit and he built the pilgrimage church and hostel as well as a bridge over the Oja River, which we would cross tomorrow as we left town.

When we arrived at the refuge some of our other friends were already there. The office was on the first floor and the sleeping area was upstairs. This place has large cubicles, each with four bunks. Margaret, George and I took one cubicle.

Matias had hidden Samba in the cubicle next to us. Some of the refuge managers took the job very seriously and watched everything very closely. Other managers would sign everyone in and then leave. Matias and Samba were lucky today, the manager didn't even come upstairs.

In the next room there was a big kitchen with a couple of large tables and lots of chairs. Some of us gathered there to drink coffee and talk. Alejandra, Auxi, Jacinto, Lourdes and several of the others bought their food at the local grocery stores and fixed their dinners in the evening in order to keep their expenses as low as possible. They were getting ready to eat and, of course, they always invited us to eat with them, even though we had not contributed anything. We always declined and said we would go out to eat. We usually had to eat later because the restaurants didn't start serving very early. We would usually go out for a hot chocolate or a beer and kill some time until the restaurants opened, but today George had to doctor Margaret's feet and that took any extra time we had.

DAY #11

▼

—SANTO DOMINGO DE LA CALZADA TO BELORADO, 14 MILES

The refuge in Belorado was managed by Rudy Snell and his wife. They belong to the Swiss Society of the Friends of St. James and they were there for two weeks of volunteer work. Rudy had retired from his job a few months ago and he told me they had walked the camino and had wanted to come back and help in one of the refuges. The Swiss society sponsors the refuge in Belorado and provides a little funding.

The refuge was part of one of the churches which was no longer in use. The church was locked, but Rudy had the key and he asked me if I would like to look around inside. He took me in and told me all about the church.

There was another large church no more than a hundred feet from this one. I asked him why they had built two huge churches so close together. He said he really did not know, but he thought the second one may have been built in a period when the camino was at its peak and there were many pilgrims to accommodate. As we were walking through the church I mentioned that Matias was also from Switzerland.

He said, "I know. I talked to him and I told him Samba could stay inside overnight. You don't object to that do you?"

"Oh no! That's fine with me. Samba is a good dog. She never makes any noise and is not a problem at all," I replied.

"Well, it is very much against the rules," he continued, "but I told him it would be okay if no one complained."

The Snells had even given Samba an official pilgrims pass.

Even though the Snells had welcomed Samba, she was not welcomed by everyone. That evening Matias was playing with her in the kitchen and dining room area.

An older Spanish woman said to Matias, "I don't think you should be playing with the dog in the kitchen."

Matias then calmed Samba down and the Spanish lady did not make a big fuss about it.

The refuge here was small. There was a kitchen with big wooden tables and benches on the main floor. The showers and bathrooms were also on the main floor. There were two small bedrooms upstairs and in each room there were five double bunks with a very narrow aisle between them. The only natural light in the room came in from a tiny window which was so high you could not see out of it.

It had turned cold and there was no heat in the rooms. Margaret had gotten a couple of blankets from the Snells, but she thought she was still going to be cold. I had thermal underwear in my backpack which I had never used. I thought I might need it toward the end of November. I offered the thermals to Margaret and she accepted gladly.

When sleeping in such close quarters, besides all the snoring you never knew what other weird sounds you were going to hear during the night. Someone must have been having a nightmare, because in the middle of the night I was awakened by a scream, and then everything was quiet again. I could not determine who it was.

Day #12

▼

—Belorado to San Juan De Ortega, 14.3 Miles

When we got up this morning we could not tell what the weather was like, since we could not see out our window. I was dressed before everyone else so I volunteered to go downstairs and check the weather. I went outside for just a couple of minutes to breathe in the fresh air and found that it had rained during the night and it was now very foggy, but it was not cold at all.

Last night, in the refuge, we had met three women from England. One was a nurse and the other two also worked in health services. While we were taking a rest they came by and, even though they did not appear to be real friendly, they talked to us for a couple of minutes and then continued on their way. Auxi and Jacinto also passed us.

As we were walking Margaret said, "Wow! Did I have a nightmare last night! I dreamed that a man was trying to crawl into my bed!"

"Was that you?" I laughed. "I heard someone scream, but I didn't know who it was."

Just before noon it began to rain again. We stopped and put on our ponchos. We were nearing highway N120 again and we hoped it would quit raining before we had to walk on the road.

We were not so lucky. It continued to rain pretty hard as we started walking on the highway toward the oncoming traffic. There were a lot of trucks today and when they were passing each other in the rain and fog we were afraid they might not see us, so we had to stay alert every minute in case one of them was taking up part of the shoulder.

We finally stopped in Villafranca Montes de Oca for lunch. Auxi, Jacinto, David and Anthony were already there. In addition to working on Margaret's feet last night, George also tended to a couple of blisters for Anthony. He was a Spaniard and we had met him for the first time yesterday.

We had our lunch there and killed some time hoping the rain would let up, but this proved to be one of those dismal days of only rain and no sun.

While we were in the coffee shop, Alejandra, Frederic, Vincent and Guillaume arrived. They said they were going to stay there overnight. Their feet were wet and since they were just now healing they did not want to take the risk of getting blisters again.

Alejandra said Matias and Samba were staying an extra day in Belorado. Matias wanted to take a day off so Samba could rest her feet. The refuge managers were not supposed to let pilgrims stay more than one night unless they were sick, but the Snells were very reasonable people and they didn't hold with those strict rules, especially if the refuge was not crowded. After all, what harm could it do?

. We continued on to San Juan de Ortega. It was a primitive little village with just a few houses, the church and one café. The refuge was part of the church and was run by the priest. There was a small reception area in the priest's quarters, which was also a part of the church. In the reception area we noticed a small sign saying, 'the cost for staying in the refuge is 300 pesetas ($2), and for that price do not expect first class accommodations!' That didn't sound like a very warm and friendly welcome.

When we rang the bell an elderly gray haired man came out into the foyer with the registration book. Margaret began to sign the book when she turned and said to me, "Bob, there's a column on here asking for your age!"

"Margaret," I said, "I don't think it'll make much difference if you fib about it."

I signed the book next and just couldn't resist looking to see what Margaret had written down as her age. 'Forty? She's really pushing it back!!', I thought. As we signed in, the man advised us that mass was at seven o'clock and the door to the refuge is locked at ten o'clock.

In order to get into the refuge itself, it was necessary to go outside again, walk just a few feet, and go in through two large doors. This was another ante room, except it also doubled as a garage. There was a small car parked in here and a couple of benches were against the wall. Auxi and Jacinto were sitting on the benches. I'm not sure if the man who registered them said anything or how her opinion had been formed, but Auxi did not have a good feeling about this place.

"I do not like this place at all. These people are just acting too weird for me. I'm not sure if we are going to stay," she said.

"Where will you go?" I asked.

The next refuge was several miles away and it was beginning to get dark. It would really be difficult to walk in the dark, because much of the path here goes through the forest, and with all the rain there are many mud holes which you can barely get through even when you can see the whole path clearly.

Auxi said, "I think we can find a place to stay in Ages."

I assumed she meant a hostel, because my German guide book did not indicate that there was a refuge in Ages. Anyway, they decided to walk on because they did not like San Juan de Ortega.

We went upstairs to check out the refuge. As we walked up the stairs we saw another sign, 'respect the rest of everybody with your silence!' There were two large rooms with thirty beds in each. A single bare light bulb, hung from the ceiling in each room. The washroom was not very clean and there was neither hot water, nor toilet paper. There was no heat and it was going to be cold tonight. It had rained all day and the clothes we were wearing were either damp from rain or sweat. I thought, 'this looks like it's going to be a wonderful night.'

When Margaret saw the bunks, she exclaimed, "There aren't any blankets! I can't stay here in the cold without a blanket!"

At this late hour it was obvious that we couldn't walk any farther and there was no other place in the village to stay.

"Let's go back downstairs," George said, "and I'll ask them if they have a blanket that you can use."

George and Margaret went back to the registration desk and knocked on the door. The priest's housekeeper, an elderly gray haired woman, opened the door.

George told her that Margaret needed a blanket and asked if she had one she could use. The housekeeper said she had only one blanket and she would give it to her later.

They thought that was a curious attitude. Why couldn't she give them the blanket now?

Margaret didn't want to push her luck and aggravate the housekeeper so they left and went next door to the cafe. The café was immediately next to the church. It was after six o'clock when we joined David, Anthony and the three English women there.

There were only eight of us staying in the refuge that night. The café was very small with two tables. It had started to get cold so the little wood burning stove, which was going full blast in one corner, took the chill out of the room. All of us welcomed the warmth and we pulled the tables closer to the stove. We gathered around the tables and drank wine and beer, while we discussed the conditions in this refuge.

David and Anthony had been talking to the woman who owned the café. Apparently, for quite some time, there had been a feud going on between the priest's housekeeper and the café owner. She told David and Anthony that the priest did not heat the refuge because he thought pilgrims should suffer on the way to Santiago.

George said, "Oh, just walking 500 miles isn't suffering enough, huh? Do you have to sleep in the cold too? Well, I'm going to fool him. I've got a good sleeping bag!"

As it approached seven o'clock Margaret started to make rumblings about going to mass.

George said, "I told you I can't possibly go, because I made a solemn promise to St. James that I wouldn't go to mass before I got to Santiago."

Margaret thought the housekeeper was holding back the blanket for a reason and she said, "Oh George, you're just being difficult!! If we don't go to church, she may not give me that blanket!"

In order to make a good showing, the three English women and I agreed to go to mass with Margaret, but George, Anthony and David couldn't be budged from that warm stove.

The church was very big for such a small village. The village was named after St. John of Ortega, who was born nearby in 1080. He was the principal helper to St. Dominic and built churches, hospitals, roads and bridges. He also offered spiritual help to pilgrims. His tomb was in the center of the church.

When we entered the church there were already two people present. The priest's housekeeper was sitting on the far left side of the aisle and the café owner was sitting on the far right side of the aisle. When the church bells began to ring, a gray haired man came out from behind the altar and began to say mass. It was the same man who had registered us when we arrived. There was no sermon, no one took communion, and the mass lasted about fifteen minutes.

As the evening grew on it became colder and it had been terribly cold in the church. We went back to the café to sit by the fire and get warm.

I had read in my guidebook that the priest offered homemade garlic soup to all pilgrims in his residence at eight o'clock every evening. Margaret said she had also heard about that and she was sure the priest expected us to be there for soup. I said I thought it would be nice to go, just out of common courtesy, but no one else was interested in going.

It was just about eight o'clock when Margaret and I knocked on the door of the priest's residence. When he came to the door, he said, "Are there only two of you?"

I immediately sensed some disappointment and I quickly said, "I'm sure that more are going to come."

I whispered to Margaret, "I think you had better go back to the café and see if you can talk some of them into coming over here. He doesn't seem very pleased about the low turn out."

In a few minutes, Margaret returned with George, Anthony and David.

She said, "I had to beg all three of them to come! I told Anthony, 'If you want George to work on your feet again, you had better get over there!'"

All of us sat at the table in the kitchen while the housekeeper stirred the big pot of soup she had on the stove. She tasted it a few times and finally thought it was ready. She passed out a metal bowl to each of us, and then filled it with soup. It was very good.

While we were eating our soup, the priest came in and started talking to us. David and Anthony were Spaniards so, of course, they spoke the language. George had learned a lot of Spanish so he could also talk to him. My Spanish is rudimentary and so was Margaret's. We just sat and listened.

During the conversation, two troopers from the Guardia Civil, the Spanish State Police, walked into the kitchen.

The Guardia Civil was formed in 1844. They patrol the countryside and always travel in pairs. They usually know what's going on in their territory and they make it their business to know about the movements of strangers or foreigners.

In 1936, when the Spanish Civil War started, many of the Guardia Civil, who were stationed in those provinces in which the Republicans had strongholds, were murdered. They gravitated to Franco's side and have remained an intimidating peace-keeping force even up to the present time. The tricorn, or three-cornered patent leather hat which they wore, became a symbol of authority. Within the last twenty years they have discontinued wearing that hat, in order to soften their image, and now only use it for ceremonial purposes. They have also traded in their horses for BMW motorcycles and Ford Broncos.

It appeared as if they dropped in at this refuge frequently, because the priest and the housekeeper seemed to know them pretty well. They were also given soup and while they stood there eating they were making casual conversation with us.

They were asking questions such as, 'Where are you from? Are you travelling with anyone else? Have you been to Spain before?'

We didn't know if they were asking these questions to be friendly or if they were looking for someone. As soon as George said he was from Brazil, one of the policemen began speaking to him in Portuguese. Was that to see if he really was from Brazil?

The Guardia Civil either command a lot of respect, or are feared. David and Anthony seemed nervous with the policemen around and couldn't wait to get out of there. Maybe it was due to our own ignorance that George, Margaret and I did not find them intimidating.

As soon as they had finished their soup, David and Anthony went back to the cafe. While all this was going on George found a hair in his soup and Margaret was elbowing him in the ribs warning him to keep his mouth shut about it. She was sure that everything had to go just right or she would not get the blanket. She finally asked George if he would talk to the housekeeper once again about the blanket. George did ask and the housekeeper went and got one blanket and gave it to Margaret. As soon as we could graciously exit the place we did so.

Earlier we had asked the café owner if she would make something for us to eat that evening. She made omelettes and french fries for all of us. David and Anthony had told her about Margaret's difficulty getting a blanket and she offered a sleeping bag which she had. These places never open early and Margaret was concerned about returning the sleeping bag the next morning. The woman told her to just put it on the bench in front of the café. Throughout Spain I found that people were exceptionally friendly and this was just another example. The woman and her husband made all of us feel very welcome in the café as if we were regulars.

After dinner we went back to the refuge. I checked the thermometer on my backpack and the temperature in there was 54 degrees.

George insisted on taking a shower every night, no matter what the conditions were. As he went to the washroom, he said, "If you hear someone screaming tonight, it'll be me stepping into the shower."

Just before ten o'clock that evening, as George was doctoring Margaret's blisters and I was holding the flashlight, we heard loud steps on the stairs. A key was slid noisily into the lock and turned, all the lights went out, and then we heard steps going down the stairs.

Margaret said, "Can you believe that? He has locked us in!"

Day #13

▼

—San Juan De Ortega to Burgos, 18 Miles

Because this was going to be a very long day, we left while it was still dark, but the sky was clear and it was not raining. As we passed the café Margaret put the sleeping bag on the bench.

We used our flashlights to find our way to the path. The track was through the woods and there were bushes and small trees on both sides of the path which made it difficult to get across some of the mud holes. It was slow going until we came out of the forest.

Shortly we came to the small village of Ages. I was walking a little ahead of George and Margaret when I saw a dark haired girl in her pajamas taking some clothes off the line. I thought it was extremely unusual to see a Spanish girl outside in her pajamas.

She saw me coming and waved to me, and shouted, "Hello!"

I was even more astonished! I waved back and said, "Hello."

I passed just a few yards farther on and stopped to look back as George and Margaret approached.

The girl said, "Oh hello," and she gave George a hug.

Then I finally realized who it was. It was Lourdes. I had not expected to see her here and I didn't recognize her in pajamas and without her glasses. Her grandfather lived in Ages and she and Dominick had stayed there overnight. She said Auxi and Jacinto had also stayed there. Now I knew why Auxi felt so sure she could find a place to stay in Ages. Auxi and Jacinto had left already and Lourdes and Dominick were leaving very soon.

The village of Atapuerca is just a short distance away. There are a lot of caves in the Sierra de Atapuerca. It was here in 1992 that archeologists found some prehistoric human remains. Some scientists now believe that 'Atapuerca Man' is possibly the earliest example of man in Europe.

There was a café in the village where we could get breakfast. We had already walked about four miles so we were very hungry. Auxi, Jacinto, David and Anthony were already there enjoying the usual breakfast of coffee, bread, butter and marmalade. We joined them at their table and ordered the same.

We were discussing the long walk to Burgos, when David, who had walked the camino before, said, "The last four or five miles are not very pleasant. You are walking through industrial areas, car dealerships and small manu-facturing plants."

I suggested to Margaret that she should take the bus when we hit the suburbs of Burgos to save her feet a little.

She said, "Why don't the three of us take a taxi? It won't cost very much!"

I was teasing her when I replied very seriously, "Margaret, I'm not worried about the cost, I was thinking of my conscience."

She scoffed, "Oh, tell me about your conscience! Someone who has to be dragged to church shouldn't worry about taking a taxi a few miles!"

Just a few minutes walk from Atapuerca, after climbing a fairly steep hill, Burgos can be seen, about 14 miles away. We stopped and enjoyed the view. We were able to pick out the most dominant structure, the huge cathedral.

It was three o'clock in the afternoon when we reached the suburbs of Burgos. We saw a big restaurant where we thought we could telephone for a taxi. After dealing with a lot of traffic we finally worked our way across the busy road. A woman called a taxi for Margaret. While George and Margaret had a coke I used the telephone to call home.

Burgos is a large city with a population of about 160,000. The city was founded in 884 and became a principal commercial city being at the crossroads of the routes leading from the sea as well as being on the Camino de Santiago. Today Burgos is a city bustling with commercial activity. You can see this as you walk across the town. There are numerous factories and other businesses.

The Gothic cathedral of Burgos is one of the most magnificent in Spain. Construction was started in 1221 and it was consecrated in 1260. Today it is being sandblasted to remove centuries of soot.

El Cid Campeador was one of the most famous residents of the city. He played an important role fighting the Moors and advancing the re-conquest of Spain.

After the taxi took Margaret away, George and I started walking again. I didn't think the outskirts were as bad as David had portrayed them. There were a lot of businesses and car dealers, but there was a wide sidewalk on which to walk.

We walked for a long time and finally were in the city. The refuge was on the other side of town so we had to go all the way across Burgos and from the time we began it took nearly four hours. As we were approaching the entrance to the park in which the refuge was located, a taxi began blowing its horn. The occupant was Margaret.

"Hi guys," she said. "I don't have any change. Can you loan me some?"

I had plenty of change so I gave her a couple of dollars for the taxi. She got out and walked with us to the refuge. She had been downtown and had taken her clothes to be laundered. She said they were going to be ready about nine o'clock that evening. She said if we wanted to take our clothes in there they would have them ready for us in the morning. We thought that was a good idea.

She also commented, "Oh, by the way, those English girls beat you guys to the refuge."

I was surprised. I didn't see them pass us and I was wondering how they had done that.

The Burgos refuge was a new one and it was located in the middle of a park. There was a military hospital across the road from the refuge. Margaret had learned that a doctor there administered to pilgrim's feet at no charge. She was planning to go there and ask him to look at her feet.

We said we would meet her there after we got situated in the refuge and we would bring our clothes to take them to the laundry.

Margaret called a taxi from the hospital and we took it downtown. We found the laundry and gave them our clothes. The young man who was working at the counter said they would be ready at nine o'clock the next morning.

The laundry was in the old part of town and in that vicinity there were a lot of places to do some shopping. Both George and I needed to buy underwear and he also wanted to buy socks and sock liners. Margaret took this opportunity to buy some wool socks so she could get rid of the cotton ones. The socks and sock liners were the same brands which I had bought before leaving home. I was surprised at the price, which was about fifty percent more than I had paid.

It was starting to get late and we still needed to have our dinner. There were dozens of places to eat. It was just a matter of picking out one which we thought would provide the fastest service.

We found a place which had a lot of tables and provided quick meals.

While we were eating, Margaret said, "I was talking to that Dutch girl. She walks about twenty five miles a day!"

"Well, sure!" George said. "Did you see her legs? She's got legs like a horse! If I had legs that long, I could walk twenty five miles a day too."

The Dutch girl was about six feet tall and, at first glance, it did appear that the majority of her body consisted of legs.

"And that Swiss girl, you know which one I mean, the one that passed us on the trail today," Margaret continued, "she has a tiny backpack. When I mentioned how small the backpack was, she said, 'Well, I'm carrying a lot of invisible baggage!'"

George asked, "Do you think she would agree to carry my backpack tomorrow if I offered to carry that invisible baggage for her?"

The fact that those English girls had beaten us to the refuge still bothered me and I said to Margaret, "I still can't figure out how those English girls beat us to the refuge. We didn't stop much today. We were walking our legs off and I never did see them pass us, unless they passed while we were waiting with you for that taxi."

"Oh, I forgot to mention it. They took the bus from the suburbs," she said casually.

"Well, why didn't you say that? Here you had me thinking that we were really slow."

She laughed, and said, "Oh, I wouldn't say you guys were slow, but I've never heard of you passing anyone."

We quickly finished our dinner and paid our bill.

We walked out to the street and began to look for a taxi. The sidewalks were loaded with people. It was about ten o'clock, which is still early in Spain. At that time of the evening a lot of people are just beginning to think about dinner.

The refuge closed at ten-thirty so we took a taxi in order to get back before closing time.

DAY #14

▼

—BURGOS TO HORNILLOS DEL CAMPO, 12 MILES

For a donation of about seventy cents we were served coffee with bread and butter in a small maintenance building next to the refuge. The building had a dirty stone floor and was full of old machinery and junk, as well as the long wooden table at which we sat.

While his two big dogs wandered around inside the shed an old man prepared the coffee in a large pot and poured each of us a cup along with hot milk. It really was not very good. After taking my first sip, I spat it out.

"What's wrong?" George immediately asked. "Was it a hair? Tell me, I can take it!"

"No, it wasn't a hair," I replied. "The milk had curdled on the top of my coffee, and I got a mouthful of that."

The English women said goodbye to us. They had finally become a little friendlier. They were going to take a train to Bilbao to see the new Guggenheim Museum and then return to England.

We had to go back downtown to retrieve our laundry which was supposed to be ready at nine o'clock. Margaret, Auxi and Jacinto accompanied us. Auxi and Jacinto were going to the bank. George, Margaret and I had our backpacks on, while they did not. They were going to come back to the refuge to pick up their backpacks.

We decided to take the bus downtown. After a couple of stops the bus was getting crowded and, although we were standing, it was especially awkward for us because we had our backpacks. Most of the passengers were elderly people. They probably did not realize that Auxi and Jacinto were with us because they were not carrying backpacks. Jacinto said some of them were grumbling because the bus was so crowded and they were making comments about how terrible it was that pilgrims were riding the bus. I guess they thought we were cheating. I told George it was too bad we couldn't make a general announcement that 'we're just going back downtown to get our laundry!'

Our laundry, of course, was not ready. The young girl who was doing the laundry and ironing said it would be ready at eleven o'clock. We had less than twelve miles to walk that day, so if we started about noon, we would still be okay. We took this opportunity to find a decent café and have a real breakfast.

The laundromat was in the old part of town where the streets are narrow and winding. There are many places to eat here. Just a few doors away we found a nice place which had been extensively remodeled. There was fine wood paneling on the walls and fancy stools for sitting at the counter. There were numerous good things to eat lined up on the counter. We sat there and enjoyed a good cup of coffee and some pastries.

After breakfast we wandered down to the main square and sat there for awhile to kill some time before heading back to the laundromat.

Most things in Spain are cheap, but having your laundry done is not. It cost $14 to have one bundle of laundry washed and ironed. In that bundle I had one pair of pants, an undershirt and two long-sleeved shirts. George had just a little bit more than that.

I had washed my socks by hand. I did not want to have them washed at the laundry because I was afraid they might shrink them. A few days later we would have a bundle of laundry done in Ponferrada at a cost of $21. George and I talked about starting a little business and putting washing machines and dryers in all the refuges.

We took a taxi back to the refuge. We found the path and began to walk.

There was just a little rain about noon, but after that it cleared up and the sun was shining. We were entering *La Meseta*, which extends for about sixty miles. This was farm land and it was very flat, with few trees. There was no place here to escape the sun, making it especially difficult to walk in summer because of the extreme heat. Even now, in late October, it was pretty warm.

We reached Hornillos del Campo around five o'clock in the evening. As I approached the refuge I saw a man, about forty-five years of age, sitting on a bench reading John Grisham's novel *The Chamber*.

He said to me, in excellent English, "So, here we are."

At first I thought he was English, and I said, "Hello."

His name was Hugo. He was a medical doctor from Amsterdam.

The door to the refuge was open so we went in and selected our bunks. This was also a new refuge. The Spanish government had built quite a number of these in the past few years because the walk had become so popular and they thought this promoted Spanish culture and tourism.

The manager appeared around six o'clock to register everyone and stamp the passes and collect the $3.50 cost of staying there. A young man dressed in very dirty clothes and carrying a guitar in addition to his backpack asked the manager if he could stay there, although he did not have any money. The manager said if he could not pay, then he couldn't stay there.

Auxi and Jacinto were staying here also. Auxi was having a problem with one of her knees. It was beginning to bother her. I had an extra knee brace which I had not used so I gave it to her.

When we went to dinner that night we invited them to come along. They did not seem to have a lot of money so we said we would pay. They declined and said they would fix something for themselves in the refuge kitchen. We asked them to at least come over and have coffee with us. They agreed to come to the restaurant later.

George stayed behind for a few minutes to organize his things.

There is only one place to eat in this village and it was a short walk from the refuge. As we left the refuge we saw the young man who was turned away lying in his sleeping bag on the ground next to a wall of the church. It was going to be a cold night so I suggested to the others that we might want to tell him to come inside after the manager left.

Hugo, Margaret and I were the only ones in the restaurant. We had a glass of wine while we waited for George. A very nice middle-aged lady was waiting on us and we assumed she owned the place.

This gave us a good chance to get to know Hugo. He had decided to take six months off from his practice to travel and think about his future. He had been in general practice for eighteen years and had now finished his studies for psychoanalysis and wasn't sure what he wanted to do. His wife was also a surgeon and, over the years, they had done a lot of travelling together. They got married while they were in school.

After they finished medical school they volunteered to go to Surinam for the Dutch government to work in one of the hospitals for several months serving the local population. After returning to the Netherlands they set up their own practice. They now had two teen-age daughters, one of which was in a kibbutz in Israel.

After he told me that, I asked, "Are you Jewish?"

"No," he replied, "My daughter just thought she would like to do that for a month or two. My wife is in Israel now visiting her."

After a short while George showed up with Auxi and Jacinto. He had talked them into coming with him, but they said they were not going to eat. They would just visit with us while we had our dinner.

We had taken a table for four so we pulled up two extra chairs. The owner picked up the small electric heater which had been in the middle of the room and moved it closer to our table, because it was getting a little chilly.

We ordered our food and then George asked the lady if we could have a couple of extra plates and knives and forks, which she provided. Although Auxi and Jacinto objected, Margaret and George shared their meals with them. The owner's husband showed up and helped her serve the meal. I wondered if they would say anything because we ordered four meals, but we were using plates, glasses and utensils for six meals. They did not make any comments at all about it.

Before we left the restaurant, each of us ordered a sandwich for the next day. In Spain, the tip is always included in the price of the meal, but in this instance we left a little extra for the woman, because she had been very considerate.

When we left the cafe it was pitch dark and there were no street lights so we used our flashlights to find our way to the refuge. It had now turned even colder. After checking to make sure the manager had left, we told the young man to come in and take a bunk.

Auxi put a pot of water on the stove and pulled some packages of coffee out of her backpack. She made coffee for everyone and we sat around the big table in the kitchen and talked and tried to keep warm. There was no heat in the refuge, but it was a lot better than being outside.

The young man, whom we had invited in, was named Javier. He did not have any food, so I gave him half of the sandwich which I had bought for tomorrow. I figured that I had been eating too good anyway. Since he had a guitar, I wondered why he didn't play it for everyone.

We learned that Hugo had left Amsterdam on his bicycle. It was a "Condor" recumbent bicycle, which is the type you pedal while lying nearly on your back. He had hopes of riding it all the way to Spain, but he had a lot of trouble just getting over the hills between Amsterdam and Paris so he knew he would never make it over the Pyrenees. He continued on to Chartres and left the bicycle at a hotel there and intended to pick it up when he went home. From Chartres he took a train to Bilbao to visit the Guggenheim, then to Burgos and started walking from there. This was his first day of walking and he said he already had one blister.

Day #15

▼

—Hornillos Del Campo to Castrojeriz, 12 Miles

The path today was good, a little muddy here and there, but for the most part it was fine. It was very windy and cold when we left the refuge. I was wearing three shirts, my hooded jacket, knit cap, and gloves. Although it warmed up later, it was windy all day.

This area is pretty flat and you can see a great distance across the fields. Occasionally we would see a farmer plowing with a tractor. We knew that we should be approaching the village of Hontanas and we were looking for it in the distance, but we could not see it.

After a while we could see a little smoke rising in the distance as if it were coming out of the ground. We finally came to a crest in the hill and then there was a valley and the path went down very steeply to the village. We were immediately on the main street and protected by the buildings from the wind.

The village looked like many others on the camino, a few dogs, some abandoned houses, and very few people. We had really been looking forward to a good cup of coffee, but our hopes were dashed when we found that the only cafe in the village was closed. We continued walking and within a hundred yards came to the refuge.

From the looks of the building you would never know it, but the refuge was very nice. The interior of the old building had been restored and had been brought up to modern standards. The toilet and shower facilities were especially well done.

We had not been able to get any coffee before leaving Hornillos so everyone was disappointed that the café was not open. George saw some workmen across the street from the refuge and went over to talk to them. They said they thought the owner was going to open the café in a few minutes.

George, Margaret and I anxiously walked back to the café just as the owner was opening the door. There was a big German shepherd lying on the steps at the entrance to the cafe. He turned out to be harmless.

We were very disappointed to find that the place was a miserable dump. There was a huge fireplace and firewood was scattered all over the floor. There were two large tables and a few chairs scattered here and there. The counter was dirty and cluttered. I looked over the counter and saw packages of muffins and cookies on the floor. The coffee machine was a small affair, much like one you might have in your home, not the commercial type you would expect in a café. The machine could only make one cup of coffee at a time, and it did that slowly.

I did not order any food at all. I just wanted to have a quick cup of coffee and get out of there. I took straight espresso, because I didn't trust the milk he had on the counter. George and Margaret took their coffee with milk.

The owner was a short balding fat man wearing a tee-shirt which barely fit over his big stomach and he had his glasses pushed up on top of his head, but that cosmopolitan touch didn't do much for him. At least he must have been a friendly person because he had pinned to the walls numerous pictures which had been taken during the summer with pilgrims.

While we were at the café, Auxi and Jacinto had fixed their lunch at the refuge and they joined us as we pushed on toward Castrojeriz.

Hugo had walked on ahead, but he waited for us at the edge of the town. The refuge was at the far end of the town so we still had a good distance to walk.

The manager of the refuge turned out to be a little Napoleon. After I registered, he began speaking to me in Spanish. I thought he was going to show me to the bunks, so I followed him into another room, and after putting my backpack down I realized that it was the kitchen. Apparently he was just showing me around. He continued to speak to me in Spanish. We then went to the dormitory and now Hugo and Margaret were following us.

Margaret started to say something, and the manager said, in Spanish, "Listen! Listen!"

Margaret tried to say something again, and now the manager said, in a raised voice, in perfect English, "Miss, please listen! Learn to listen, before you speak!"

I thought he was being a little harsh for no reason at all. He finished telling us, in Spanish, whatever information he was trying to convey, and then he departed. He thought all pilgrims should understand Spanish although he spoke very good English.

There were four bunks to a cubicle. Margaret and I took the two lower bunks and Hugo and George took the uppers. There was a steel beam running lengthwise just a few inches above George's head when he was lying down.

"I'm really going to have to watch that when I get up in the morning," he said.

Margaret came back from the washroom complaining that the toilet facilities were pretty bad. She said, "The door to the toilet is a saloon type door and you can't lock it. Would it be too much to ask to have a door which goes all the way to the floor and locks?"

The toilet here was pretty grim and both men and women had to use the same one.

After getting our things arranged we went out to have a drink. While we wandered around the streets we looked for a restaurant where we could have dinner that evening. We came across a small grocery store and bought a few things for the next day. I bought a large chocolate bar and several packages of coffee for Auxi and Jacinto. I gave that to them later, saying I had just bought too much and did not want to carry it.

We were lying in our bunks resting before dinner. When it was time to go, we heard a loud "bong" sound from the top bunk and some choice words from George as he climbed down, rubbing his head.

When we got to the restaurant we saw Javier sitting on the sidewalk with his hat on the ground. He was playing his guitar and asking for money. I guess that's why he was carrying the guitar. Each of us gave him some money before entering the restaurant.

Day #16

▼

—Castrojeriz to Itero De La Vega, 8 Miles

In Castrojeriz they had a loudspeaker system and we woke up to Gregorian chants. The chants were accompanied by a loud "bong" from the top bunk.

"Damn!" George said, "I remembered that beam when I went to the washroom in the middle of the night, but this morning I just forgot all about it."

This refuge provided coffee, cookies and apples for the pilgrims before leaving. That was the nicest thing you could say about this place. Other than that little courtesy, they were not very friendly.

Within a short distance from the town there was a steep hill which took you up to a plateau. As we climbed this hill the fog began to close in and the weather became chilly. We put on our ponchos just as a slight rain began to fall. Even though it was pretty cool, we were sweating a lot as we climbed toward the top in the fog and mist.

Margaret stayed behind with Auxi and Jacinto to take a tour of the church. This was going to be a short day for us. This would give us a chance to get more rest.

Hugo, George and I walked on to Itero de la Vega, arriving just shortly after noon. It was not a big place, but there were two cafes.

The refuge consisted of one sleeping room and a bath room. There were only eight bunks. We saw that the floor was messy with mud and dirt. Pilgrims, who had passed by earlier, had probably walked in with their muddy boots to use the washroom. We swept up the dirt, cleaned the washroom, and mopped the floor. We left our boots at the door and walked around in our stocking feet in order to keep the floor clean.

Two young Spaniards from Madrid arrived and asked us if there were open bunks available. We told them they could take the two bunks nearest to the front door.

We were hoping Margaret, Auxi and Jacinto would hurry up and get there because there were now only three empty bunks left. We put some of our stuff on the empty bunks so they would look as if they were occupied. Fortunately they showed up shortly after that and claimed the beds.

A short while later a Frenchman arrived looking for a bunk. He could not speak English or Spanish, but Hugo spoke French and was able to talk to him. He told him there were no beds left, but that there was a mattress in the hallway near the washroom if he wanted to use that and sleep on the floor. He gladly accepted the offer.

· He was an unsavory looking character and none of us felt good about him. We made sure we had all of our valuables in our pockets every time we went outside.

About seven o'clock, Matias and Samba appeared. Matias said Alejandra, Frederic, Guillaume and Vincent were following him and would arrive shortly. Lourdes and Dominick also appeared. We told them there were no more beds.

We thought we would be staying a day ahead of them and we asked Matias why they had walked so far today. We thought their feet really must have gotten a lot better.

Matias said all of them had gone into the refuge at Castrojeriz, but the manager, the little Napoleon, was very nasty to them. He was especially offended when he learned that Samba had an official pass. Matias said the manager shouted, "It's sacrilegious for a dog to have a pilgrim's pass!"

All of them decided to leave and walk on to Itero de la Vega, making their walk for the day a total of eighteen miles.

After learning that there were no more beds, Alejandra and Auxi went across the street to the cafe and asked the owner how to get in touch with the manager of the refuge. He said the manager lived nearby and that he would telephone him.

Within about thirty minutes the manager drove up with his wife and children accompanying him. Auxi told him there were a lot of people who needed beds.

He said there was an empty floor in the next building which they could use for shelter, but there were no beds. They would have to sleep on the floor and there were no toilet facilities. They would have to go outside and come into our building to use the washroom. So now we had seventeen people using one washroom.

Before the manager arrived Matias hid Samba under one of our beds. George took his poncho and put it over her. She was very still all the time so she was not noticed. Those precautions turned out to be unnecessary. The manager didn't even enter the refuge so there was no chance that she would be discovered. Samba was going to sleep inside tonight.

There was no restaurant in the town where you could get a complete meal. The café only served drinks and small appetizers, but Alejandra and Auxi talked to the owner and negotiated a deal with him whereby he would provide a hot meal for us.

He agreed to make ham and eggs for all seventeen of us. He said his mother would do the cooking, but everyone had to have the same thing because he had neither the food nor the cooking facilities to serve everyone specially requested dishes.

We put all the tables in a row so all of us could eat together. His mother could only make two plates at a time so before the last people got served, the first ones had already finished eating.

Wine was served as part of the dinner package. Wine just didn't seem to go with ham and eggs. Just about everyone at the dinner had started walking at St. Jean Pied de Port, so we toasted that town. It turned out to be a very nice dinner and we thanked his mother for doing all the work.

Day #17

▼

—Itero De La Vega to Fromista, 10 Miles

It was a restless night for me. I went to the washroom three times and my back felt as if I had spent the night on a torture rack. I got up early and went outside for some fresh air. I saw Vincent sitting on a bench reading his Bible. Of the three Frenchmen, he was the most religious. He was interested in looking at every church along the way.

After everyone had gotten ready to go, we went back to the cafe across the street and had magdalenas and coffee.

My original schedule had called for us to walk thirteen miles to Poblacion del Campos. There was a very small refuge in that town, but there was no place to eat. Margaret asked me if we could just walk to Fromista because that's a pretty big town and there are several places to get a hot meal, and she said she felt much better when she could get a hot meal in the evening. We all agreed that we would stop at Fromista.

The path and the weather both were great today. The weather was breezy and the temperature was about 65 degrees.

When we got to Boadilla del Camino we stopped for a hot chocolate. The Church of the Assumption in that village is worth visiting so Margaret, George and Hugo decided to stay an extra few minutes and take a look at it.

I was suffering from culture overload so I decided to walk on to Fromista. This walk of four miles to Fromista turned out to be the only time on the whole trip that I walked entirely alone.

The path continued along an old canal. The canal was on my right and on my left there was a long row of beautiful white poplar trees with golden leaves. Many leaves had fallen on the path which made the walk even more enjoyable.

Just before I reached Fromista I met an American woman walking alone toward me. We stopped and talked for a short while. She was probably in her late fifties. She had already walked to Santiago and had a few days left to kill before returning home, so she was walking back to Burgos. She was from California and had a new granddaughter that she was anxious to see.

I continued on and within a few minutes I was in Fromista. I followed the yellow arrows toward the refuge. About half a block before getting to the refuge, I saw Lourdes and Dominick sitting on a bench.

As I approached them, I asked, "Aren't you going to the refuge?"

"We were already there and we looked it over," Lourdes replied. "The place is not very nice. Also, Javier is there and he's very drunk. I think we are going on to Poblacion del Campos. Would you tell Auxi and Jacinto that we went there?"

"Sure," I said. "I'll let them know."

I went on to the refuge. It was a two-story structure with a couple of large rooms on the first floor and four smaller rooms on the second floor. I climbed the stairs to the second floor and looked around. Javier was in one of the rooms. No one else was around. There was a shower and toilet on this floor and they looked pretty clean. I picked one of the empty rooms which had six bunks and put my backpack down on one of them. Other than the dirty mattresses, the place didn't really look too bad. I think that some of the others had been worse.

Maybe Javier was the reason Lourdes did not want to stay. There were only two blankets in the room and they looked very clean. I picked up the blankets, folded them, and put them under my backpack. I knew that Margaret would be looking for blankets and I did not see any more.

I went back to the bench where I had met Lourdes and Dominick. They had already left for Poblacion. I waited there until George, Hugo and Margaret arrived. I told them about my conversation with Lourdes, and told them I didn't think the refuge was that bad.

Margaret said, "Well, I was thinking about staying in a hostel tonight anyway. There is supposed to be a pretty good one here and I'm kind of tired of those refuges."

"Maybe I'll stay in a hostel tonight too," Hugo said.

"What do you want to do George?" I asked.

"I'll take a look at the refuge," he replied.

"Why don't we meet back here in about an hour and go for a drink," Margaret said.

"That's a good idea. We'll see you guys back here in a little while," I replied.

George and I walked back to the refuge and Margaret and Hugo left to find the hostel.

In front of the refuge we saw the two young Spaniards who had stayed with us in Itero De La Vega last night. One of them seemed to be having problems with his feet. We talked to them for a while and found out that one of them was having severe cramps in his legs and he was giving serious consideration to quitting and going back to Madrid.

After George had looked over the refuge, he put his backpack in the room which I had taken and said, "It's not bad at all."

I pulled out the blankets which I had hidden and gave one to George. "Here," I said. "I guess Margaret won't be needing these so why don't you spread one out over your mattress because they look a little grim. I'll use the other one."

While we were getting settled two Spaniards and one Frenchman entered the room. They asked us if we would mind if they stayed with us. We, of course, said that would be fine.

They put down their packs and began to take out those things which they were going to need that evening. After washing up and getting settled in they decided to go out for a drink.

A short while later, Matias entered the room. "Would you guys mind if Samba and I stayed here in your room tonight?" he asked. "I'm next door with Javier and he's not only drunk, he stinks something awful."

"Sure, you can come in here," George said. "There's one bunk left."

While I was taking a shower, I heard a commotion in the hallway and I thought, 'I'll bet the manager found Samba and he's kicking Matias out.'

When I came back to the room I was pleasantly surprised to see that Matias and Samba were still there.

"What was going on out here?" I asked.

George said, "Those three guys came back and when the two Spaniards saw Samba they said they wouldn't sleep in the same room with a dog."

"I offered to move downstairs," Matias said, "but they said they preferred to move. The Frenchman really didn't care if Samba was in the room, but he went with the other guys."

George and I walked over to the tourist office to get our passes stamped. While we were there we saw Auxi, Jacinto, Alejandra and the French guys coming into town. I told Auxi what Lourdes had said about going on to Poblacion. She was a little surprised because she said she thought all of them were staying in Fromista tonight.

Alejandra and the Musketeers said they would also go on to Poblacion if Auxi and Jacinto went there. Auxi said she and Jacinto didn't have any choice because Lourdes had all the food which they had bought to share in her backpack.

I told Alejandra that Poblacion was pretty small and there are only a few beds.

"Well, I slept on the floor last night, so one more night won't make any difference," she said.

George said, "Isn't that just like Lourdes? She makes a decision about where to stay and goes on without even discussing it with Auxi. Of course Dominick does whatever she says, so she didn't have to discuss it with him."

We met Hugo and Margaret in front of the church. Nearby we had seen a very nice restaurant in an old mansion. We decided to go there for a drink.

It was an ancient place with a lot of antique wooden furniture and paneled walls. There was one room with nice tables and big comfortable chairs. The price for dinner was about three times what we usually paid, but it was much too early for dinner anyway. At that time we were only interested in having a drink and relaxing for a while. Hugo treated us to a round of beers and we enjoyed a good conversation.

"I really like this place," said Margaret. "At least it isn't filled with smoke."

"Doesn't everyone in Europe smoke?" I asked.

"Well, I haven't seen Hugo smoking, and I'll bet his daughters don't smoke," she said.

"Margaret, I'm sorry to disappoint you, but one of my daughters smokes, and I even enjoy having a cigarette now and then," said Hugo.

"You're kidding me! And you're a doctor!" she said.

"Oh, I know it's not healthy to smoke, but I figure that she could be doing a lot worse things," Hugo said.

After we had finished our drinks, we went to Hugo and Margaret's hotel and sat in the lounge watching television until it was time for dinner.

We had seen a couple of restaurants as we had entered the town so we walked over to one of them that had been recommended by the two young fellows from Madrid.

The place was very busy with a bar on the main floor and a dining room upstairs. We saw the Spaniards who had moved out of our room. They were having dinner with some other pilgrims and did not see us.

We walked with Margaret and Hugo back to their hotel, said goodnight and then went back to the refuge. When we entered Matias was sitting on his bunk working on his feet. We sat and talked for a while before getting ready for bed.

Matias said, "While all of us were out, someone stole the fruit that I bought for tomorrow."

George said, "Well, my binoculars are missing too. I wasn't going to say anything, because I thought maybe I had lost them."

"No, you didn't lose them, George," I said. "They were hooked to your backpack when we went over to the tourist office. I saw them and I thought maybe I should put them away, but then I dismissed the idea thinking no one around here would take anything. I guess I was wrong."

"There's only one person around here that I might suspect," George said.

"Javier!" Matias and I replied, in unison.

"I don't guess I can go over there and accuse him without any proof," he said. "I guess that will just be a lesson for me!"

Day #18

▼

—Fromista to Carrion De Los Condes, 12 Miles

The path was excellent today, the surface consisted of finely crushed stones and it was very easy walking. Occasionally we would see a concrete pillar about three feet high with a ceramic plaque embedded in it. The plaque had a bright yellow shell painted on a bright blue background. The shell was the symbol of the camino. Now and then the plaque would be missing, a victim of a souvenir hunter.

"The people who take those plaques have to be driving, or on a bicycle," I said.

"That's for sure," said George. "Those things must weight about a pound and walkers are looking to throw things away, not pick up more things to carry."

"You can probably buy those in the souvenir shops in Santiago," I said.

On the way we stopped at the refuge in Poblacion. Most of our friends were still there. I walked through the place and saw that some of them had to sleep on the floor, but it looked as if they at least had mattresses. Lourdes and Dominick had already departed.

The path ran alongside a road, P-980, all the way to Carrion. The weather alternated between hot and cold depending on whether or not the sun was out.

At Carrion there was a private refuge run by Catholic nuns. The Monasterio de la Santa Clara was an old convent and only about ten nuns were still in residence.

After ringing the bell, a voice over the intercom asked if we wanted to stay there tonight. After replying in the affirmative, a nun presently appeared. Her name was Sister Maria Leticia. She stamped our passes and collected $7 from each of us for a room.

She took us upstairs and as we followed her, she asked, "Are you a family?"

"No," George replied, "but we have been walking together for several days."

There were three bedrooms with two beds in each and one larger room with four beds.

She pointed to the larger room and said, "You can take this room if you like."

After the nun departed, Margaret said, "If one of those other rooms is vacant tonight, I'm going to take it and then you guys can snore all you want."

As George sat down on his bed, he said, "This is just like home. I've got a little table next to my bed on which

I can put my glasses. I haven't been used to that kind of luxury lately."

The room defied description. It was not square. It was sort of rectangular, but not exactly. None of the four walls were the same length and the ceiling was so low that Hugo, at just over six feet, had to be careful not to bump his head on the light.

The sheets were perfectly clean and the blankets were the heaviest that I had ever seen, but we knew it would probably get cold during the night so we still used our sleeping bags.

At the end of the hallway there was a nice bathroom with a modern shower. The kitchen was downstairs and was at our disposal if we wanted to use it. There was also something in the kitchen which you rarely see in Spain, a coffee vending machine.

Margaret found something she didn't like about the place. While we were outside waiting for the nun to come downstairs and let us in, she spotted a strip of wax paper in front of one of the doors. The paper was about three feet long and about eight inches wide. There was a sticky substance on the paper and five mice were stuck there. Four of them were dead, but the fifth one was still struggling for his freedom. The sticky substance apparently was poisonous.

"I know those nuns make and sell cookies here," she said. "Remind me not to buy any."

We walked to the downtown area to do some shopping. While I was standing in a shop doorway trying to decide which postcards to buy, I heard "Chicago, Chicago, Chicago."

It was Lourdes, Dominick, Alejandra and the Musketeers coming down the street. They told me they had checked into the refuge and it was small, but they were happy with it because there was a nice kitchen where they could fix their own food.

All of us gathered at a small café a few doors away and drank coffee and talked.

George had been wanting to try Poncharin, a liqueur which is made from blue berries, such as those which we had seen on the trail. As we walked, George would quite often stop to pick berries, acorns or anything else which looked different and interesting. He kept a small cheese box in which he stored his collection.

He was especially interested in the blue berry. We had seen the bottles with a picture of the blue berry on the front and he wondered how it tasted. He tried one of the berries when we were walking and he said it tasted awful. "Maybe that's why the birds won't eat them," he said.

He bought three small glasses of the liqueur and passed them around the table so all of us could take a sip. He was wondering how they could have processed those awful sour berries into something which tasted so good.

There was a grocery store next door to the café. We bought some orange juice, meat, cheese and bread to have for lunch tomorrow along the way. Tomorrow we had to walk a ten mile stretch with no places to buy food and it would be very difficult for this team to go that far without eating.

Day #19

▼

—Carrion De Los Condes to Calzadilla De La Cueza, 10 Miles

When we left the monastery that morning, it was a cold 39 degrees, but the cold weather did not dampen Hugo's enthusiasm. He started singing one of his favorite songs, the theme from the TV show *Rawhide*. That was one of the things which we liked about him. He was always in a good mood and he would make all of us laugh when he scrunched his hair up on his head and put on a face which reminded us of Stan Laurel.

George was not used to this cold weather and had never seen snow. He was always worried about that. I told him, "It will get warmer when the sun comes up."

He wasn't convinced, and replied, "That's what one mammoth said to the other just before they froze. Some of the guys were saying there is snow falling to the west of Leon."

"I didn't hear anything about that, George. I think they are just trying to scare you," I said.

A couple of blocks from the monastery there is a cafe which doubles as the bus station. It was open early so we stopped for our coffee. Of course, all the other walkers were there too.

The path today was across flat land and not very scenic. This must be a terrible place to walk in July and August when it's hot because there are no trees at all, only open fields all around. Some farmers were still working in the fields as we passed. One of the crops was sugar beets and we saw several wagons loaded with them. I often wondered if the farmers made a decent living here.

We were walking along a small dirt road when a white bronco-type vehicle came up behind us. It was the Guardia Civil. Usually two troopers travelled together, but today there were three of them in the vehicle and the one in the passenger seat was holding a cell phone. They stopped and rolled down their windows.

We walked up to the vehicle and they asked their usual friendly questions about where we were from and if we were walking with any other friends. They did not ask for any identification and after a few minutes of casual talk they continued on their way.

About noon we found a picnic table and benches alongside the path. We stopped and spread out all the food we had bought. We had ham, cheese, bread, tomatoes, a tangerine, a couple of croissants and some apples.

George had also bought a small can of mussels. Hugo and I tried one and George ate the rest. They tasted better than they looked.

We had been walking for a long time and we kept looking for the village, and although the land was relatively flat here, we could not see anything in the distance. With each small hill that we came to we thought that when we got to the top we would see it, but all we saw was more road. Margaret was now having a problem with one leg and she and George were far behind me. Hugo had gone ahead and was about ten minutes in front of me. I finally reached a crest in the road and could see some smoke coming up from the area to the left of a tower in the distance. After walking a little further I began to see the roofs of houses. Calzadilla de la Cueza was now just ahead of me.

I could see Hugo waiting at the edge of the village. It was a small place, only about a dozen houses, one café and a new pilgrim's refuge. Hugo had already checked everything out. A man in the local café had the key to the refuge.

There was an old refuge here which was in terrible shape and it had been closed when they built the new one. The new one could accommodate forty people. It was a much better refuge than most although it was not heated. Another big disadvantage was the absence of a kitchen. Because there was no kitchen, Auxi and the rest of our friends continued on to Ledigos which was about three miles farther.

One of the men at the café seemed to be acting as the hospitalero. He had the key and he took Hugo and me back to the refuge, stamped our credentials and gave us two blankets for Margaret. It was cold during the walk today when the sun was not shining. Hopefully it wouldn't be too cold tonight.

The manager showed us some sinks in the back yard which we could use to wash clothes. He said we should make sure we kept the door closed because the mice would try to get in if we left it ajar.

As we walked today we saw thousands of holes in the sides of the ditches where field mice lived. Occasionally you would see a mouse running from one hole to another. They must be real pests for the farmers. I wondered what methods they used to keep down the rodent population.

I washed some socks in the backyard while Hugo, Margaret and George sat in lounge chairs and watched a family of field mice running back and forth across the ground. I hung the socks on the clothesline to dry. Later that night I brought them in and pinned them to my backpack even though they were not dry, just so I wouldn't forget them.

There was absolutely nothing to do in this place except sit in the café and drink coffee, beer, or hot chocolate, and watch television. While we were sitting in the cafe, the owner and his wife disappeared and went upstairs and left us alone. We caught up on a late afternoon soap opera which we had seen before. George was the only one who could understand what they were saying, but we watched it anyway.

While the owner and his wife were upstairs two more pilgrims came in. They wanted coffee, but we told them they would just have to wait until the owner appeared again. They sat at one of the tables and waited for about half an hour before the owner came back.

They did not start serving dinner until eight o'clock so we had quite a bit of time to kill. I wrote out several of the postcards which I had bought and got them ready to be mailed.

It was five minutes before eight when Hugo made an attempt to go into the dining room. The manager stopped him and said it would not be open for another five minutes. It's amazing how important they think it is to be punctual about their special hours for dinner, when many other things are done with such a carefree attitude.

From time to time we met strange characters on the camino. We met one here. He was one of the two pilgrims who had come in while the owner was upstairs. He was a Spaniard and he carried a small briefcase and nothing else. He and a German pilgrim sat at the table next to us. They were not friends, but had just been walking together for the last couple of days. The Spaniard was talking to us, in Spanish, while we were trying to eat. Hugo and George understood him fairly well. He was talking about mystical things on the camino and what a great religious experience it was to walk the ancient path. He was going on and on about this as we were eating. He must not have planned to walk for many days, because he only had that small briefcase in which he carried whatever he needed.

We were glad to finish our dinner and get back to the refuge. The Spaniard and the German pilgrim were the only other people there that night, and fortunately, the weird one didn't continue the conversation in the refuge.

We went to bed at nine-thirty because there wasn't anything else to do. It was now getting colder and, in addition to the two blankets, Margaret was wearing all of her clothes to keep warm.

Day #20

▼

—Calzadilla De La Cueza to Sahagun, 14 Miles

I was awakened by some loud talking.

"I don't know about you guys, but I'm getting out of this damned place!" Margaret shouted.

I realized right away that Margaret was in a foul mood.

"What's wrong?" Hugo asked.

"What's wrong?" she replied. "My blankets are damp, my clothes are damp and I'm freezing my ass off! That's what's wrong! You guys can roll over and keep on snoring if you want to, but I'm getting out of here!"

"Bob, what's the temperature in here?" Hugo asked.

I looked at the little thermometer which I carried on my backpack and said, "Looks like 47 degrees. That's pretty cold."

Margaret continued, "You're damned right it's cold! I'll bet those rats, being in their cozy warm holes, are even better off than we are. I'm not even going to wash up. I'm going over to the bar and I'll brush my teeth in a cup of *café con leche*!"

Hugo, George and I joined her at the café a short while later. She was having coffee with the usual breakfast and we could see that she was in a much better frame of mind. We had our breakfast and after Margaret had a second cup of coffee she was perky again and ready to hit the trail.

The sun was up already and there was only a slight breeze. It was beginning to warm up a little. The path was very good and easy to walk and by ten o'clock the temperature was 55 degrees.

Occasionally we would meet someone who was walking east rather than west toward Santiago. On this day we met a young French girl, very pretty, about 25 years old, coming toward us.

"You're going the wrong way," I jokingly said.

"I know," she said, "I've already walked to Santiago, and now I'm on my way back home."

"Where are you from?" Hugo asked.

"Lyon, France," she replied.

"Wow!" Hugo exclaimed. "How far is that?"

"From Lyon to Santiago and return it's about 2,000 miles, " she answered.

"And how long have you been walking?" I asked.

"I left my home in July and I expect to get back there sometime in January," she replied.

"May I ask why you're doing this?" I inquired.

"I just love the camino," she said. "It is just a joy for me and I am happy when I am walking here."

Hugo and I went on our way and a few moments later we looked back and saw that she stopped and talked to George and Margaret for just a minute and then continued on.

Margaret was probably also wondering why a young girl would be doing that. Margaret was not planning any super long distance walks. Her leg was still causing her a lot of pain. I suggested that she take the train tomorrow from Sahagun to Leon and rest there for three days. Today was Thursday and we would be in Leon on Sunday and we could meet her there. She could start walking again with us on Monday. She said she would think about it because her leg was now beginning to hurt a lot.

At the refuge in Sahagun we found that they did not have blankets so Margaret decided to go to a hostel which was run by some nuns. George walked over there with her.

The refuge here was built recently using a portion of the old church. They used the original walls and put on a new roof. The ceiling was about thirty feet high and pigeons had found their way inside and had built nests in the rafters. It would be best to take a lower bunk here.

I sneezed several times in this place and for the first time since I began walking my allergies were bothering me a little. I'm not sure if it was because of the pigeons or not.

There were eight large cubicles in the dormitory and in each cubicle there were eight bunks. This was a very roomy place. There was no shortage of space here.

Hugo said he would shop for groceries and he would make dinner for all of us tonight. I had already seen a nice bakery down the street so I offered to buy the dessert and Margaret said she would bring a bottle of wine.

For dinner Hugo made omelettes with potatoes, onions, and green peppers. With our meal we had wine and bread and for dessert we had cream rolls.

Earlier in the evening I had asked the young girl at the reception desk if she had a train schedule. She did not have one, but she called the train station and got the schedule for trains going to Leon. The train takes a little over thirty minutes to go from Sahagun to Leon. It would take us three days to walk the same distance.

I gave the schedule to Margaret and she discussed my suggestion with Doctor Hugo to get his opinion. He told her it was a good idea, because her leg was definitely not going to get any better if she kept walking on it.

She decided to stay over in Sahagun for two nights and go to Leon on Saturday. We agreed to meet her in Leon in front of the Convento de las Benedictinas at four o'clock on Sunday. I don't know how we ever decided on that as a meeting place. It proved to be a bad idea.

Margaret offered to take our dirty clothes with her to Leon and have them laundered. Hugo and George decided to take her up on that offer, but I was a little concerned about it so I declined. I just did not want to take the chance of losing any of my clothes.

They walked with Margaret back to her hostel after dinner. George said she seemed a little sad when they left her.

There was only a Spanish couple, probably in their thirties, staying in the refuge with Hugo, George and me. She was very pretty. He wore small glasses and had curly hair which was graying a little.

They were sitting at the kitchen table along with me as I updated my journal. Hugo and George had already retired for the night. He had a small flute and was practicing his music as softly as possible while they sat there.

Day #21

▼

—Sahagun to El Burgo Ranero, 12 Miles

It was a very comfortable night. The temperature was 60 degrees in the refuge when we got up that morning. I was still sneezing and my nose was running.

During the night we had a little company. We had left a pad of butter on the counter in the kitchen. A small hole had been chewed through the side of it.

As we were trying to find our way to the path we saw a farmer driving down the country road on a tractor. We stopped him to inquire if we were going the right way. He said that we were and he continued on a few hundred feet where he crossed a tremendous mud hole which completely covered the road. It was going to be difficult for us to get around it. After he had crossed he realized that it would be a problem for us so he backed his tractor up through the water and mud and told us to get on. Hugo jumped on the rear and George and I climbed on each side of the tractor and the farmer drove us through the mud and water. On the other side he stopped and we got off. We thanked him and then he went on his way.

As we approached Bercianos, a small village, there was a herd of sheep on the right side of the path. We had learned that when you see sheep you should look for dogs as well. A large dog was attending to the sheep and was standing guard at the edge of the trail. We were walking three abreast at that time and we wondered if the dog was friendly.

The dog was stretching and yawning so I said, "It does not look as if he's paying any attention to us."

He suddenly took notice of us, let out a loud bark, and ran in our direction. He circled around us, but didn't make any more aggressive moves.

I said, "Let's just try to ignore him."

"That's very difficult when he has his teeth in the leg of your pants," George said. George was just kidding and the dog finally went back to the sheep and left us alone.

We reached El Burgo Ranero around two o'clock in the afternoon. The village consisted of a few dozen houses, some of them abandoned. There were two restaurants, but both of them were permanently closed, undoubtedly from lack of business, and there was no one on the streets. It reminded me of some of the small towns in southern Illinois in which I had lived as a boy, where a day could seem like a week, and most of the people eventually died of boredom.

The refuge was in the center of the village and the door was unlocked. We went in and made ourselves at home.

We selected our bunks and then went into the large sitting room where there were two big tables and a fireplace, but no wood.

We were glad to see that there was a washing machine and a dryer in the kitchen. I took advantage of this to wash my walking pants and some shirts.

While my clothes were drying George and I went to the local bar and had a cup of coffee. The place was filled with tobacco smoke. A young man was waiting on the half dozen customers who were there. They were all men, smoking one cigarette after another, and playing the slot machine.

We thought that it would be nice to build a fire at the refuge.

George asked the young man at the bar, "Is there any-place where we can get some wood for our fireplace?"

"No. There's no place to get any wood," he replied. "All these houses heat with oil. But if you see some wood lying around, just take it."

We didn't think we were going to see any wood lying around in this town, so George decided to go back to the refuge and I took a walk around the village. I discovered that there was one dark grimy little grocery store and a pharmacy in town.

As I was walking I met a young Brazilian couple, Luis and Christine. They were looking for the refuge. I took them back with me and introduced them to George and Hugo.

While walking I had seen the Fonda Pension Lozano and thought we might be able to eat there. We did not have any food with us and there was no place else to eat. Later Hugo, George and I went over there and spoke to the old woman who owned the inn. She was very friendly and welcomed the chance to make some money.

When we asked her if she could fix dinner for us that evening she said, "Of course, I would be glad to." She quoted a price similar to what we had been paying for meals. Being as she was so agreeable, we asked her if we could eat a little early, possibly at seven-thirty, and she said that would be fine.

On our way back to the refuge we saw some old wooden pallets behind the building. George and I broke some of them up and passed the pieces through the window to Hugo.

He got the fire started and had it going pretty good when the manager came by. He stamped our passes and collected the $2 fee for staying there. By now more pilgrims had arrived.

The flute couple and an elderly Brazilian couple, Jose and Maria, had shown up. Jose was 75 years old and his wife Maria was 65. He did not look as if he were in great shape, but he was walking every day without any problems. He carried wine in his canteen and his wife carried water in hers.

Jose was a Spaniard who had left Spain when he was 28 years old and had gone to Brazil. It was in Brazil that he met and married Maria, who was Portuguese. This was his first trip back to Spain.

George was talking to Luis and Christine and learned that walking the camino was Luis' idea. His family owned a small furniture factory in Brazil and he worked for his father. He said he was pretty stressed out by that and he thought this would be a good way to get away from everything for a while. Chris was not as happy. She had not prepared very well for this long distance walking and her feet and legs were hurting her and they did not have real good sleeping bags so they were cold quite often during the night. She was anxious to finish and get back home.

We returned to the inn at seven-thirty and the lady had a nice meal prepared for us. She showed us to one of the three small tables in her dining room. The food was served family style. There was wine, soup and salad, plenty of meat and potatoes and for dessert we had the choice of apples or peaches. The cost was about $7 each.

Day #22

▼

—El Burgo Ranero to Mansilla De Las Mulas, 12 Miles

It was a bad night for me. My back was aching. It was probably because of those beds, and too much time in them.

In order to easily locate my flashlight I had gotten into the habit of putting it in my right boot overnight. I fished it out and got up in the middle of the night and went downstairs to the dining room where I could turn on a light.

I sat at one of the big tables and brought my journal up to date. Some of the embers in the fireplace were still glowing and providing a little heat. There were large windows in the room and I had a good view down the main street of the village. The wind was blowing, but other than that nothing was happening. Not one car passed during the hour I sat there.

I was not looking forward to walking tomorrow without any sleep so I finally went back to my bunk.

We usually went to bed every night by ten o'clock, because the lights were turned out at that time, and we got up at seven o'clock. I was always up earlier than that, but I didn't turn the lights on until then. When I got up this morning, I had to slowly get myself out of bed, taking great care not to hurt my back.

The first thing I did every morning was tape up my toes, heels and arches. The micro-thin tape seemed to be working so I wanted to stay with that routine. I used my flashlight to do this in order not to disturb those who were still sleeping.

At noon it was 65 degrees and sunny with a cool breeze. The path was great for walking. The land was still flat here and you could see far in the distance. The other pilgrims who had stayed at the refuge were also on the trail. The flute couple walked very closely together and seemed to be having some serious conversations. Luis and Christine were in front of us and Jose and Maria were a few yards behind us.

We left the refuge at nine o'clock and arrived in Mansilla at two-thirty in the afternoon. After finding the refuge and getting our gear stowed away, we wandered around the town. There really wasn't much to look at. We did find a café that made hamburgers and had one with a large plate of french fries.

We found a small grocery store and replenished our supply of candy bars, apples and other snacks. Hugo offered to make breakfast for us in the morning so we also bought cocoa, milk, cheese and bread.

A very friendly and helpful young woman, about twenty-five, was the manager of the refuge. When she came to the refuge that evening she had her younger sister and a small dog with her. After she stamped our passes I talked to her about the refuges between there and Santiago. I wanted to know which ones were closed at that time of year. She went through the whole list and told me the good points and bad points about every refuge between Mansilla and Santiago. She spoke pretty good English, but would get mixed up sometimes. She apologized, saying that everyday she had to speak Spanish, English, French and German to the pilgrims and sometimes she couldn't think of the right words.

DAY #23

▼

—MANSILLA DE LAS MULAS TO LEON, 11 MILES

It was cold last night. When we started walking this morning it was 45 degrees. My fingers were getting a little cold even with my gloves on, but by eleven o'clock it had warmed up enough for us to take off our jackets.

The flute couple had also stayed at the refuge and we saw them again today on the path. Once again they were having some intense conversations as they walked and were not paying any attention to anyone else around them. We didn't know what was going on with them, but it looked as if they were having some arguments.

Just a mile or two from Leon we were once again stopped by the Guardia Civil. They talked to us for just a few minutes and then told us to be careful walking on the highway and then they left.

Leon is a big city with about 200,000 population. The refuge was located near the center of town so we still had a long walk after entering the city.

As we walked through the outlying neighborhoods George said, "Hey guys! Do you see that?"

"See what?" Hugo asked.

"That sack over there. That's a McDonalds sack! We are back in civilization again."

The pilgrim's refuge was on the third floor of an old gray four-story building. It looked as if it had been an army billeting place at one time. The outside appearance was deceiving because it was pretty nice inside. There were huge washrooms, separate ones for men and women. There was a long hallway and the rooms were similar to hotel rooms, except that there were eight bunks in each room. Luis, Chris and the flute couple were in the same room with us.

During the last hour of walking Hugo began to experience a lot of pain in his shin. He decided to rest while George and I went out to look for McDonalds.

"Hugo, after we go to McDonalds, George and I will walk on into the center of town and meet Margaret," I said.

"Yeah, go ahead," he replied. "I'm going to rest here for a while to see if my leg gets a little better, then I'll meet you guys in front of the cathedral."

George and I found the McDonalds restaurant and had lunch. It was a big place, with seating for 200 people. It was well maintained and I asked the manager if it was new. He said no, but they were building another one in Leon and it's going to be even bigger.

It looked as if business was very good here because this one was packed.

After lunch we walked on into the center of the city. We did not have a good map and we got lost several times. It was difficult to find anything in the old part of the city if you were not familiar with the streets. They were extremely narrow and winding.

George and I wandered around for an hour looking for that Benedictine monastery. There were a lot of people on the streets and we finally stopped five young people, in their twenties, and asked directions.

They did not know where it was either, but they were more than willing to try to help us. One of the young girls and one of the boys spoke a little English. They walked with us and eventually we did find the place, but it was no longer a Benedictine monastery.

Although we were half an hour late getting to our appointed meeting place we waited for a little while expecting Margaret to show up.

While waiting, we were talking to the young people who had helped us. One of the girls offered me a cigarette, which I declined. They knew that there was a big campaign in America against smoking. It seems as if everyone in Europe smokes. They said that even in Spain there will soon be a campaign against smoking.

After talking to us for a while the young people went on their way and we walked to the cathedral. There are many cathedrals in Spain and a list of the most beautiful ones would surely place the cathedral in Leon near the top.

The city of Leon gets its name from the word 'Legion' because the city was originally a military garrison for the Romans at the time of Christ. The city has been occupied by Romans, Visigoths and Moors. In the 8th century the city was taken back from the Moors and was reoccupied by Spanish Christians. Work on the cathedral began in the 12th century on a site which had previously been occupied by Roman baths. It is a masterpiece of Gothic style and contains more than 100 stained glass windows.

When we arrived Hugo was sitting on a bench in the cathedral plaza.

"Where's Margaret?" Hugo asked.

"We finally found the meeting place, but we were late, so maybe she went back to her hotel," said George.

"She called my house and gave my wife the name of the hotel, so I'll call her," Hugo said.

We saw a coffee shop across the street and while we had a cup of coffee Hugo used his cell phone to call Margaret's hotel. After a long time someone finally answered and connected him with her. She said she would come over and meet us.

· Within a few minutes Margaret was peering in the window of the coffee shop.

After hugs all around, George said, "Hey Margaret, we waited in front of the monastery for you."

"I called Hugo's wife the other day and I asked her to tell him to call me at the hotel," she replied.

"She must have forgotten to tell me that I was supposed to call you," said Hugo.

"That's okay," George said, "we're all back together again now."

"Have you guys been doing okay?" Margaret asked.

George said, "We've been doing fine. We just had a great lunch over at McDonalds."

"I hope you didn't gorge yourself on that junk food!" she exclaimed.

"Well, now let me think for a minute," he paused and then, just for effect, said very slowly, "I had a Big Mac, a large order of fries, a chicken sandwich, a large coke, an apple pie, and a strawberry sundae. I love McDonalds!"

"Oh, George, that's disgusting!" she said.

"Margaret, how is your leg now, after that rest?" I asked.

"It is much better. And look at my feet," she said proudly, showing off a new pair of boots. "I bought new hiking boots and they feel great. Do you think I should have gotten brown instead of blue?"

"Don't worry," I said, "after all the mud and cow manure we're walking through, they'll be brown by the time you get to Santiago."

"How is the hotel, Margaret?" asked Hugo.

"Oh, it's terrible! Those owners are very inefficient," she replied. "You were lucky that they even answered the phone. There is a family consisting of the husband and his wife and her father who are running the place and they are just not organized at all. I hate to tell you guys, but I'm having trouble getting the laundry done. I looked for a laundromat, but there just isn't any. So I asked the woman at the hotel if she would launder the clothes and she agreed to do it. She said she was doing clothes for other people and she would take care of it. As of a couple of hours ago the laundry still wasn't done yet. Maybe she has it finished by now."

After looking around in the cathedral, we walked over to Margaret's hotel. It was a small place but there was a nice waiting area with a couple of sofas and chairs. We waited there while Margaret asked for the woman who was doing the laundry.

She was probably in her thirties, and she looked tired. She had just come up from the basement, where the washing facilities were.

George explained to her that they wanted to pick up their laundry. She was trying to be as friendly as possible, but it was obvious that she was under a lot of stress. She said that all of it was not finished yet.

George was being very polite and said that was okay, they would just take it anyway. She made at least six trips downstairs and back up, bringing clothes. Half of the things she brought up belonged to neither George nor Hugo. She seemed to be terribly disorganized and frustrated. I felt sorry for her because she was trying to do her best.

They finally took all the clothes they could identify. Hugo got all of his clothes, but George lost a tee-shirt and a pair of socks.

After the laundry fiasco was finished, Margaret said, "I found a couple of cyber cafés near here. Would you guys like to go over there and try to get on-line to check your e-mail before we go to dinner?"

I said I wasn't too interested because I had heard that getting connected was awfully slow, but both Hugo and George wanted to try it anyway.

Margaret lead us to one of the cafés, but it was so crowded there were no terminals available. We went to the other one which was nearby. Computers were available there. The café was filled with teenagers and the air was filled with smoke so I said I would go down the street to a different place and have a drink while I waited for them.

Margaret said, "Bob, I'll go with you. I can't stand this smoke either."

A few doors away we found a cafe. It was crowded because there was a soccer match on the television. Some small children had accompanied their parents and everyone was watching the game. Margaret and I squeezed through the crowd to an empty table and ordered a couple of beers.

Soccer is as popular in Spain as football is in America so a lot of people go to the cafes to have a drink and watch the game and talk to their friends. Some of the places become more like social clubs than cafes.

After more than an hour Hugo and George came in and told us they never could get a satisfactory connection to check their e-mail or to send any mail.

We found a restaurant and had something quick to eat. At dinner Hugo said he thought that he would take the train to Villadangos, which was our next town, rather than walk because the pain in his leg was getting worse. Margaret said if Hugo was going to take the train she would too. They agreed to meet at the train station the next morning.

Margaret walked back to her hotel. Because it was getting late, and we did not know what time the refuge closed, we decided to take a taxi. The streets were crowded with people and it took us several minutes to hail one down. I appreciated the ride because my legs were really tired and beginning to ache. We must have walked five miles just in the city of Leon.

As soon as we entered the refuge we ran into Frederic and Guillaume. They had already walked to Astorga, but had taken a bus back to Leon in order to go to the post office tomorrow morning to pick up some money which was being wired to them. They would then take the bus back to Astorga and continue walking.

They told us that Matias had quit at Villadangos because he was having trouble with his knees. And we had always thought Samba would have foot problems and not make it to Santiago.

It was 300 miles from Villadangos back to the French border and I later wondered, many times, how Matias managed to return all that distance with Samba since the dog was not welcome on buses or trains in Spain.

DAY #24

▼

—LEON TO VILLADANGOS DEL PARAMO, 13 MILES

Because Leon is such a big city there was no problem this morning finding a good place to have breakfast. After a couple of cups of coffee and two croissants, George and I walked up one of the main streets by the river. It was very pleasant walking in the morning sunshine up the wide tree-lined promenade. The city crews were out sweeping the leaves off the sidewalk and cleaning up the weekend litter. Everyone was hurrying to work this morning so the traffic was heavy.

The yellow arrows took us to a big bridge which crossed over the Bernesga River. Adjacent to the bridge was the Monastery and Hostel of San Marcos. Its origin goes back to 1151 when it was built as a church and hospital for the poor and the pilgrims travelling to Santiago.

Today it is a five star parador in the government's chain of hotels. At $200 per night, most modern day pilgrims do not stay there.

After crossing the bridge we walked for a long time through busy little streets which gradually changed from upscale stores to repair shops, supermarkets, and road construction projects.

As we were walking George brought me up to date on one of the couples we had been observing.

"The flute couple must have split up," he said.

"What makes you say that?" I asked.

"I overheard them talking this morning," George said, "and she told him she was taking the train back to Madrid, and he could do whatever he wanted. They were not acting very friendly and I don't think they are married. I saw them at the cathedral yesterday when we were there and they weren't talking to each other."

We walked near the highway most of the day and reached Villadangos around four o'clock that afternoon. We could tell from the registration book that Hugo and Margaret were already there. After George and I signed in and selected our bunks we located them sitting in the back yard of the refuge enjoying the sun.

They told us of a nice restaurant in town and we went over there for a hot chocolate just to kill some time. They did not start serving dinner until eight o'clock so we had quite a bit of time on our hands.

After an hour or so at the café we went back to the refuge and I took that time to clean up and to get my journal up to date.

Although it was hot during the day the wind came up and the weather began to turn cold early in the evening.

When we walked back to the restaurant we had to bundle up against the cold wind.

That night, Hugo and George slept in their sleeping bags with their knit caps pulled down over their ears. We found a couple of blankets for Margaret and I loaned her my sweatshirt.

Day #25

▼

—Villadangos Del Paramo to Astorga, 18 Miles

According to my schedule we were supposed to make this a short day of only seven miles to Hospital de Orbigo, but Margaret's new boots, which she bought in Leon, were making her feel very comfortable and confident.

After three miles, she said, "Why don't we go all the way to Astorga?"

We had talked about this a few days ago, but had dismissed the idea because both Margaret and Hugo developed problems with their legs.

"Astorga is more than eighteen miles," I said. "Why don't we wait until we get to Hospital de Orbigo to decide about that because we will have gone four more miles. It really should be up to you and Hugo. I think I can make it. What about you, George, how do you feel about it?"

"I think I will be okay," he replied.

"We'll discuss it with Hugo when we catch up with him," I said.

Hugo had walked on ahead of us and when we reached Orbigo we looked down one of the small side streets and saw a backpack leaning against the wall at the entrance to a cafe. We knew right away that it was Hugo's.

We found him sitting in the café and he had already started his lunch.

"I couldn't wait for you guys," he said. "I was getting hungry."

We also ordered, and fairly quickly we had a nice meal in front of us. It was a family place and while the mother made the food the son took care of the service. After the meal the mother brought out a plate of homemade cookies for us.

While we were eating we discussed the possibility of continuing on to Astorga which was a little more than eleven miles away. Both Hugo and Margaret felt that their legs were up to it. After a big meal like that all of us felt pretty confident so we decided to walk on to Astorga.

In Orbigo there is a famous bridge on which many violent confrontations have taken place. In 452 there was the battle between the Swabians and the Visigoths and in 900, the clash between the Moors and Alfonso the Great. On this beautiful sunny day we spent a few minutes admiring the bridge and taking pictures.

The path had been good up to this point, but after Orbigo it turned ugly, very rocky and hard on the feet. The bottoms of our feet were really taking a beating with every step.

After fifteen miles, Margaret said, "My leg is starting to hurt again. I think that this is my limit. Remind me of this the next time I want to walk farther."

"We still have more than three miles to go," I said.

We dragged into Astorga at seven o'clock that evening. It was already dark. We had been on the road for eleven hours, but we did take that long lunch break.

Astorga is another important city on the pilgrim's route. It was a colony of the Asturians and their seat of justice, but it is not definitely known when people first settled here. During the Roman occupation the city was called *Asturica Augusta*, from which its current name is derived. As early as the 3rd century it was the seat of a bishop. The city's Cathedral of Santa Maria was consecrated in 1069, but it has been rebuilt a couple of times since then.

The most famous and striking building in the city is the Bishop's Palace. It was built between 1889 and 1913 and caused a scandal in the Catholic Church. The bishop at the time was a Catalan and Antonio Gaudi, also a Catalan and the designer of the still unfinished Familia de Sagrada Basilica in Barcelona, was a friend. At first glance you can recognize it as Gaudi's work. The Church was embarrassed by its opulence and closed it. It was opened many years later as a pilgrim's museum.

During the 14th and 15th centuries many ships from the Americas arrived at the Atlantic seaport of La Corunna, in Galicia, to unload their goods. Astorga was on the main route from La Corunna to central Spain and many of the muleteers were natives of Astorga. One of the main imports was cocoa and a number of chocolate factories sprang up in the city to process the cocoa. Even today,

Astorga is known as the chocolate capital of Spain and the chocolate here is supposed to be the best in the country.

We found the refuge, near the east entrance of the town, and it was crowded. When we arrived several bicyclists were sitting in the reception area waiting to be given permission to select bunks. Because we were walkers we had priority over the bicyclists. We had, fortunately, arrived before eight o'clock at which time the manager usually let the bicyclists start taking bunks.

I selected a lower bunk and Margaret took the one above me, while George and Hugo took the two across the aisle from us. There were even some triple bunks in this room. At eight o'clock they allowed the bicyclists in and some of them had to take the triple bunks. It was a job just to climb into bed if you got one of those.

There was a washroom with one toilet and shower for the men and a washroom and one toilet and shower for the women, but because of the lack of hot water, two people could not be taking a shower at the same time. Most of the refuges which we had stayed in had no heat, but this one did, and a lot of it. It was so hot I could not stay in my sleeping bag. I had to sleep on top of it.

About one o'clock in the morning I went to the washroom. I had gotten into the habit of checking to see if there was toilet paper. There was a new roll here. At four o'clock I went to the washroom again. The new roll of toilet paper had disappeared. Now I knew that it was the pilgrims who were stealing the toilet paper. It wasn't that the refuges were being cheap and not supplying paper.

DAY #26

▼

—ASTORGA TO RABINAL DEL CAMINO, 12 MILES

Astorga has a beautiful central plaza. It was obvious that the town was still prosperous. You could see that the old buildings facing the plaza were being renovated and, within them, nice modern apartments were being constructed.

We had gone to one of the little cafes on the plaza the night before for beer and olives. It was a well appointed place with a lot of wood and brass. We returned to the same café this morning for breakfast, but it did not open until eight-thirty. We sat on a bench in the plaza until the manager arrived.

The manager had gone by the bakery and he was carrying a big bag loaded with fresh bread and croissants. After a couple of cups of coffee and freshly baked croissants we started on our way.

As we found our way out of the city we passed the unmistakable Bishop's Palace and the Cathedral of Santa Maria. Restoration work was going on at the church. It was not unusual at this time of year to see a lot of restoration work because there were fewer tourists as the weather got colder. I thought to myself that this was an attractive town and that it might be worth another visit someday.

Hugo had gone on and was now a couple of blocks ahead of us. George and Margaret were walking slow today so I was a few steps in front of them. After a while I looked back and did not see them. I stopped and waited for a few minutes and they finally reappeared, stepping out of a store. The town's reputation for chocolate finally got the best of George. He had to stop and buy some candy bars.

The walk to Rabinal was fairly easy, but it was hot today and there were not many trees for shade. We passed through the village of El Ganso in which I saw one black cat and three dogs. That was the only life visible.

George, Margaret and I found some stone benches in the cool shadow of the old deserted church and took a rest there. Hugo had already walked on ahead. As we sat in the shade the three dogs came around to beg for food. They were friendly and posed no threat to us. George still had half a chorizo (salami) sandwich so he began to feed the dogs. He tore off little pieces and made them jump up and take turns getting their food.

We arrived in Rabinal around four-thirty. We stopped at the Nuestra Señora del Pilar, an old monastery, which was now a private refuge. Margaret looked the place over and she didn't like it. She was going to look at the Gaucelmo Refuge, which was run by the English Confraternity of St. James.

"Margaret," I said, "that girl, who was managing the refuge in Mansilla, told me it was closed for the winter."

"Well," she replied, as she walked away, "I'm going to see if it is really closed. It's supposed to be a nice place."

George and I paid our $3.50 to the nun and she stamped our passes. As we signed the book we could see that Hugo had already checked in. There were two rooms in the monastery, one had ten beds and was immediately next to the combination kitchen and dining room which also had a fireplace. The other room was larger, but had a very high ceiling and would be much colder. The only positive point about the larger room was that it was close to the bathroom.

After about half an hour Margaret returned, but by now all the beds in the smaller room had been taken. Sure enough, the Gaucelmo Refuge was closed so she had gone on to the only hostel in town. She checked out the hostel, but she said they were asking far too much for a room.

She was able to get a couple of blankets at the monastery so she took a bunk in the larger room. Jose and Maria, the two elderly Brazilians, were also in that room.

If you were not fixing your own dinner, there was only one place to get a meal in the village and that was at the hostel. It was about eight o'clock when we walked over there. It was a clear night, the wind was blowing and it had turned very cold, but the air smelled fresh and the sky was full of stars. As we looked back toward the east we could see the lights of Astorga, twelve miles away.

The hostel was reminiscent of a country inn. It was rustic, with a big stone fireplace and ancient wooden tables and chairs and a dusty stone floor. The fireplace was blazing away and keeping the chill out. A couple of dozen pieces of wood were stacked nearby.

Several other pilgrims were also having their dinner. We saw the young Brazilian couple, Luis and Christine, as well as three bicyclists from England, and a few Spaniards. The owner and his wife were kept busy cooking and serving the meals as well as tending the bar.

As usual the television was on, so we watched the news and George translated for us. He filled us in on the important events. The nightly program consisted of a few minutes of world events, news relative to Spain and the weather report. We were always interested in the weather. We kept watching for snow and hoping that, if we did run into snow, it would not be deep. Walking in snow would really hamper our ability to stay on schedule, especially since the yellow arrows were sometimes painted on rocks on the ground.

While we were eating our dinner we talked about how cold it was going to be that night. Margaret said it was really cold in that big room. Hugo offered to switch beds with her because he said he didn't mind sleeping in a cold room. He rather liked it. George and I agreed that we should switch bunks with the elderly Brazilian couple. They were very old and with their thin sleeping bags we thought it would be too cold in there for them. George said he was sure that if they stayed in that cold room the penguins (nuns) would be standing over both of them in the morning trying to revive them.

After we returned to the refuge Hugo began to start a fire while George and I went to talk to the elderly couple. They said they didn't want to switch rooms. They thanked us, but said they would be okay.

Hugo had a good blaze going when we went back to the dining room. Those people who had washed clothes hung them near the fire to dry and then we sat around and talked. Just before it was time for lights out, Hugo went to get some more wood in order to keep the fire going as late into the night as possible.

He came back disappointed, and said, "No more wood, guys. The nuns have already locked up the woodshed."

George intended to keep warm. He had his wool cap pulled down over his ears and the new scarf, which he bought in Astorga, was wrapped around his neck.

As he climbed into his bunk, Margaret said, "You're not going to sleep with all your clothes on, are you?"

"These are really my pajamas," he replied. "I just happened to wear them to dinner."

My bunk was on the other side of the wall from the fireplace, and even at two o'clock in the morning the wall was still warm from the fire.

I did not sleep well, as usual, so I got up in the middle of the night and sat in the dining room for a couple of hours reading a few pages of the novel, *The Chamber*, which I had borrowed from Hugo.

Day #27

▼

—Rabinal Del Camino to El Acebo, 12 Miles

We walked over to the hostel and had our breakfast. It was about 30 degrees. Probably our coldest day so far. After we had our coffee we began walking out of the village.

We were still going uphill to Mount Irago and toward the abandoned village of Foncebadon. That village was mentioned in Paul Coelho's book as the desolate place where he wrestled with the rottweiler which represented his sins.

For about an hour we walked narrow trails through broom and heather bushes which were about four feet high. There were so many small paths it was difficult to keep on the right trail. We finally came to LE142, a small paved road, and we began walking on that.

Just as we approached Foncebadon we saw a message scratched in big letters on the asphalt road. The message read, "Fight the Chihuahua!"

George laughed and said, "Only Auxi or Alejandra would leave a message like that!"

The village was near the top of Mount Irago. It was a windy, foggy, and cold place, but it was not totally abandoned, as our guide books had lead us to believe. We saw some workmen restoring an old house, and we noticed that a couple of other places were also being rebuilt.

We approached the young man who looked like the supervisor and asked him what was going on there. He said some families which had businesses in the larger cities nearby were renovating some of these old houses for weekend and summer homes. Maybe Foncebadon will be a thriving village again someday.

At 4,500 feet above sea level we came to the Cruz de Ferro, which was a simple cross standing high among a tall pile of small rocks. This was the famous cross on the camino where many pilgrims placed a rock for good luck. This was where George wanted to leave the rock which he had carried all the way from Brazil.

While George was finding a nice spot for his rock, two tourists drove by. They stopped and asked George if they could take a picture of him by the cross with his backpack and staff. Because he had not shaved for a couple of days the dark stubble of his beard made him look like a sinister character. (Maybe that's why the Guardia Civil were always stopping us.) But the tourists were happy with his appearance and thrilled to get a picture of a genuine pilgrim.

We trudged on toward Manjarin which was about three miles away. In the 16th century there was a pilgrim's hospital here, but today there are only six or eight run down stone buildings. It had been totally abandoned until about three years ago when Tomás and Ramón, ex-pilgrims, took up residence in one of the buildings. They had now been joined by one more man who had been helping them rebuild the place.

As I approached Manjarin, one of the occupants came out of the shack in which they were living and greeted me. I had been walking about six miles in frigid windy weather and was very cold so I appreciated the chance to get out of the wind and warm up.

They offered me hot coffee and graham crackers, which I gratefully accepted. As I stood there sipping my coffee and looking around I realized that the place didn't look any better inside than it did outside.

It was a total mess. Their beds were dirty mattresses thrown on top of some pieces of wood that had been nailed together. The floor was stone and covered with dust and dirt. It didn't look as if it had been swept for months. They had no electricity. They were powering their radio with a car battery. Both of them were pretty scruffy and highly suspicious looking characters. But the coffee was really good. I even had two cups. I was glad to see that they had throw-away plastic cups. There was a small wood burning stove in the center of the room which kept them warm.

Margaret and George showed up a few minutes after I had gotten there.

"Guys, this is a pigpen!" Margaret exclaimed.

I was hoping that none of them spoke English.

"You're right," I said, "but we're cold and the coffee's good."

As I looked around the room I could see a couple of old swords and some banners which had Maltese Crosses and other Knights Templar markings. George began talking to Ramon and he learned that Ramon considered himself to have been a Templar in a previous life.

We put some money in their donation basket for the coffee and crackers. They also stamped our passes and we then realized that this was a refuge and you could actually stay here overnight if you wanted to. I didn't think I would get any sleep here at all, since I would be sleeping with one eye open.

Margaret decided to leave. We gave our plastic cups to Ramon expecting him to discard them, but he washed them in the dishwater he was using and put them back with the other cups.

I also thought it was time to leave.

"I'm going to stay and talk for a few minutes," said George.

"Well, I'm not staying. I'm hitting the road," said Margaret.

Shortly after Margaret departed I left too, but I waited outside for George.

He was taking a long time, so I put my head back in the door and asked, "Are you okay, George?"

He said, "I'm fine. I'll catch up with you."

I started off and walked slowly, looking behind me frequently to see if George was following. I finally saw him in the distance. I walked even slower and stopped a couple of times until he caught up.

He told me Ramon had said he had a wife, a home and a car at one time, but he had given it all up to stay here in Manjarin to rebuild the village. He talked a lot about the Templars and said that in his previous life he had been a knight. He said when he was a knight he never lost a sword fight.

George said, "When he started talking about sword fighting, and I saw a couple of them hanging on the wall, I thought it was about time to go. But he wasn't stupid. He spoke Spanish using sophisticated words. He was an intelligent person. Maybe those are the most dangerous kind."

We were now walking on the road and as we rounded a curve we could see Margaret far in the distance. The road curved around a high hill. In order to take a short cut we decided to climb over the hill which was barren of trees and bushes. As we were coming down the other side we could see Margaret coming around the curve. We shouted to her several times before she could see where we were. She waved and then sat down to wait for us.

We were not far from El Acebo. We had to leave the road and cut across some rough terrain to get to the village.

As we entered the village we saw the laziest dog in Spain. We were always on the alert for vicious dogs that were not chained. This dog was not vicious. He was not even standing up. While he was barking at us he was lying on his side. He barely raised his head off the ground.

"I think he's just barking so his owner will hear him and think he's still on the job," George said.

El Acebo was another one of those typical villages in Spain where you hardly saw anyone. A few days later we would know why. From a booklet, which we picked up in Ponferrada, we learned that only 20 people still lived in El Acebo.

There was one main street with a little gutter down the middle for water to run off and George said, "When I see a tiny street like this I always get the feeling that some old woman is going to open a window above us and throw out her dishwater."

"They used to do that in ancient days, George, but I don't think they do it anymore," I said.

"I don't know," he said, "old habits are hard to break."

There were two cafes in the village. We stopped at the first one we came to. There was a nice dining room with a wood burning stove in the center. The owner motioned to us to take one of the tables nearest to the stove. A small black dog was dozing by the stove. He woke up and barked a couple of times when we came in. The owner told him to be quiet, so he went back and laid down by the stove again. We thought he acted as if he were the boss around there. He must have been something special because this was the first cafe in which I had ever seen a dog. That was not the custom in Spain.

We described Hugo to the café owner and asked if he had seen him. He said someone answering that description had stopped there, but he had walked on.

We had a good meal and talked about finding a place to stay. There was a refuge in the town, but it looked pretty bad and it was locked at the present time. We learned that there were two other places to stay, the inn where we were presently eating and the Refugio Taberna El Jose.

After we finished our meal we walked around to the Taberna El Jose Refuge and looked it over. There was no charge to stay there so George and I opted for that.

Margaret said it was a rat hole and she decided to go on to the next village and stay in a hostel. We agreed to meet her there in the morning around nine-thirty. All three of us were wondering what had happened to Hugo.

There was nothing else to do so George and I went back to the inn and had a beer. While we were having our drink we noticed some interesting pictures on the wall. George took a great deal of interest in them. The pictures of the village had been taken about five years ago and they showed that snow really did fall there, and sometimes, quite a lot. It looked as if they had gotten about a foot of snow. George was amazed and hoped we would be lucky enough to escape any snow.

We learned that the owners of the inn and the owner of Taberna El Jose had been feuding. At one time they both charged 500 pesetas ($3.50) for a bunk, but since the feud began Jose dropped his price to zero just to aggravate the people who owned the inn.

In the dining room we met a Belgian woman, probably in her late thirties, who had walked the camino three years ago. She was well suited for such an adventure. She had a boyish hair cut, looked very physically fit, and was fluent in several languages. She said the camino was so well marked now that it was too easy. She usually walked more than twenty miles per day and was looking for a greater challenge. In 2000 she was planning to spend the first three months in Siena, Italy, in order to perfect her Italian and then she was going to walk from Paris to Rome. There was an old path, but it has not been kept up and, over the centuries, most of it has disappeared.

It was here at El Acebo that we first met Fabian. He was a Frenchman, about forty years old. He readily admitted that he was trying to do the whole walk on little or no money, and why he had no money was a mystery to us. He said he had a good job with a security company. He was in a hurry because he had to go to Paris to work over New Year's Eve. The celebration in Paris was expected to be a lively one and additional security from all over the country was being called in to augment the city police. We thought he looked a little suspicious so both George and I had as little to do with him as possible. He, of course, was also staying at Taberna El Jose this night, so I kept my money and valuables close at hand.

The room was very small with only three double bunks. There was an electric heater in the middle of the room to keep the chill down, but it was also a great annoyance. There was a red light on the heater which indicated that it was on and when the temperature rose to a certain level, the heater would shut off automatically and the light would go off. The problem was that it did that every few minutes, so the light would come on, then go off, then come on, then go off. It was so dark in the room that it became noticeable and an aggravation.

Day #28

▼

—El Acebo to Ponferrada, 11 Miles

As soon as it was light we began walking. George and I were both glad to get out of there. We first went over to the inn to see if it was open. It was not. An old German shepherd was lying in front of the door.

George really felt sorry for him and asked me, "Do you think he slept outside all night?"

"He probably did," I replied. "I don't think they take them inside, but I'll bet that little black dog slept by the stove. He seemed to be well taken care of."

As we left the village we saw a monument to a fallen German pilgrim who had been hit by a car near El Acebo. His bicycle had been stood up on its rear wheel and encased in cement with the front wheel pointing toward the sky.

We had been walking on the road toward the small village of Riego de Ambros for about half an hour when we saw a taxi coming toward us. He flashed his lights and then stopped. We were surprised to see that it was Margaret. She got out of the taxi and came over to us.

"What in the world are you doing in a taxi?" I asked.

"You won't believe this," Margaret said. "There was no place to stay in Riego de Ambros so I walked all the way to Ponferrada and got there about eight o'clock last night. When I wanted to update my journal I realized I had lost it. The only place it can be is back in Rabinal. I must have misplaced it when Hugo and I changed beds. I'm going back there to get it. It's only costing me $28 round trip and if I can find my journal it will be worth it. I'm staying at Hostel San Miguel. When you guys get to Ponferrada come over there."

Margaret's feet must really be a lot better. It was 23 miles from El Rabinal to Ponferrada. Even getting in there at eight o'clock in the evening was doing great.

As we entered Riego we saw a café. We stopped in and had a good breakfast. When these small cafes were not busy it was interesting to talk to the owners about the local area.

This place was owned by an elderly couple and the woman was telling us they were very busy during the summer because many people had walked the camino. She also told us that, in their village, they had been having a lot of trouble with javelinas, which are wild pigs living in the mountains. The javelinas don't attack people, but sometimes they are destructive to the gardens and vegetation and just a general nuisance. They love chestnuts and there were many chestnut trees in this area and that attracted them. In order to discourage the javelinas from coming around there she said the villagers tried to burn a lot of the heather because that's where they liked to roam. The fire got out of hand though and burned up a lot more of the fields than they had planned.

As we walked out of the village we could see where they had burned the fields. We also saw a lot of chestnut trees, many of which were so big they must have been standing even when Columbus left on his voyage in 1492. All around the trees the ground was littered with chestnuts, the favorite food of the javelinas.

I thought this was one of the great advantages of walking rather than driving. We stopped by one of the huge trees and just admired its girth and wondered about its age. If we had been driving we would have passed it in a second and would not have given it two thoughts.

About an hour later, Margaret passed us in the taxi on her way back to Ponferrada. The taxi driver honked the horn and she waved and smiled so we assumed she had retrieved her journal.

Just before reaching Ponferrada we were casually walking through the narrow main street of yet another ancient village. We were talking and we were not paying any attention to the small gangway on our left that we were approaching. Just as we reached the gangway a huge German shepherd lunged out and barked loudly. Fortunately there was a strong chain around his neck and it jerked him back just before he was able to reach us. Both George and I nearly jumped out of our boots! We were caught completely off guard. We were not expecting that, and it really frightened us.

After the crusades the Knights Templar were a major presence along the camino. They built many churches and castles and protected the pilgrims. They built one of their finest structures in Ponferrada. It is a very large castle standing near the church and it has a commanding view overlooking the Sil River. Today it is partially in ruins, but efforts are being made to restore it. It is now the major tourist attraction in the city and that is fortunate because, other than the castle and the cathedral, there is nothing else very appealing about the place.

The pilgrim's refuge was located next to the castle, but it was locked when we arrived and was not scheduled to open until three-thirty.

Since we had some time to kill we decided to search for Margaret's hotel. We walked across the bridge and after asking a couple of young girls for directions, we found the Hostel San Miguel. We could see her sitting inside with some people having a drink. That was just like Margaret. She would talk to anyone and try to make new friends. We stayed outside because we were carrying our backpacks, and we didn't look very presentable.

Margaret came out and asked us if we would go to the train station with her. She wanted me to help her figure out the train schedule because she was going to call her daughter in Amsterdam to encourage her to meet us in Santiago.

We walked over to the train station and reviewed the schedule. From a pay phone Margaret called Jill. From the part of the conversation I overheard it didn't sound as if Jill was really excited about spending two days on a train coming down to Spain. Margaret told me Jill was going to check the schedules there to see when she could get a train.

I told George, "It sounds as if Margaret is putting a guilt trip on her daughter."

"Mothers are good at that," he said.

The manager of the refuge was a young American girl from New Mexico. She had been walking the camino and they needed someone to act as manager for a week so she volunteered. We saw Hugo's name in the book so we knew he had stayed here yesterday.

With the help of the manager we were able to find a laundry. Coincidentally, it was the Sao Paolo Laundromat. Sao Paolo was George's hometown in Brazil. When we entered we saw a large mural on the wall to our right, but it was a mural of Rio de Janeiro, not Sao Paolo. We were curious about that and the owner told us that a bar and club occupied this space years ago and the mural was left over from that time. He liked it so he just left it alone and he even kept the name for his laundromat.

As I mentioned before, having your laundry done in Spain is expensive. (But from personal experience I can tell you it's not nearly as expensive as in France). We put our dirty clothes together. I had three shirts and my walking pants and George had about the same amount. The cost was $21. It was now about five o'clock and the proprietor said the laundry would be ready at eight o'clock.

"George, why don't you ask him if he's positive?" Margaret said.

"I think we will just have to hope that it is done," I said.

On our way back to the refuge we stopped at a small bakery which also served coffee. That's a bad combination! We had two cups of coffee and several pastries. I'm not sure how many calories we consumed, but it was all great!

George and I had a fairly nice little room all to ourselves at the refuge. The washroom facilities though were
not very good. The doors to the showers and toilets were
constructed of galvanized sheet metal and it had a cold
atmosphere. No thought at all had been given to the toilets. When you were sitting down you could not close the
doors because of your knees. George told me later that he
sat sideways in order to close the door.

The common sitting room was big with a couple of old
badly worn couches and chairs. It was on the second floor
with large windows looking out upon the plaza. There was
a small stove in the middle of the room and a fire was
going. I met a young man from Canada here who had
actually stayed overnight in Manjarin, and he was quite
interested in the Knights Templar. George told him that I
knew a lot about them, which wasn't exactly true. I have
read quite a bit about them and I'm intrigued by that subject, but I just don't know enough to educate anyone else.

Margaret decided not to have dinner with us. It was
several blocks back to her hotel and she was cold and tired
so she decided to rest that evening.

We were going out to dinner at eight o'clock so we went
by the laundromat to see if our clothes were ready. The
owner had been true to his word. He was folding our
clothes as we walked in. We were able to see that nothing
was missing, which was a relief. Tomorrow it would be
nice to start off again with clean clothes.

DAY #29

▼

—PONFERRADA TO VILLAFRANCA DEL BIERZO, 14 MILES

As you leave Ponferrada you pass an ugly slag heap on your left, which is part of the electric power plant facility. It is probably fifty feet high. But after just a short distance the neighborhood drastically changes and you are walking through one of the best residential areas in the town. There are numerous huge houses which could be called mansions. They are built from brick or stone and have beautiful slate roofs and well cared for lawns and flower gardens.

The path today was pretty easy. We walked on the highway at times and also through farmland and villages.

Margaret felt like walking a little faster today so she went ahead of George and me. She waited for us in the small town of Cacabelos. She had found a nice upscale rustic inn and she suggested that we have lunch there.

"I know it's not like the rat holes you guys are used to eating in, but why don't you try something nice for a change," she said.

She was right. It was much better than what we were accustomed to. The main restaurant was downstairs, but upstairs there was an informal dining area with a fireplace, large wooden tables and high-backed wooden chairs. We sat by the fireplace talking to the two waitresses while we looked at the menu. After we had selected something to eat we chose a large table in a corner with big windows and a view over the street.

The waitress brought us little appetizers which were small biscuits with meat inside. For our lunch we had soup and omelettes. I admit it shouldn't have taken that long to select soup and omelettes, but the waitresses were pretty and friendly, and they had no other customers.

After we had eaten, Margaret said, "George, why don't you ask her if they sell those little appetizers?"

George asked the waitress and she said they didn't sell them.

"Well, then why don't you ask her if she will give us three of them?" Margaret said.

I thought Margaret was being a little pushy about this and I could see that George was a little embarrassed by it. And, anyway, the appetizers weren't that great.

George asked the waitress if she could give us three of them. She said it was no problem and went back into the kitchen to get them.

When the waitress returned, Margaret took all three of the biscuits, wrapped them in a napkin, and put them in her backpack.

The three of us had discussed the possibility of modifying our schedule at Villafranca del Bierzo and walking 18 miles to Cebrero instead of doing it in two days. The last six miles of this stretch was supposed to be difficult because it was very steep and the path was mud and rocks.

For the first twelve miles there were two ways to go, one of which was on the highway, which was the original pilgrim's path. The other way was a new path which had been developed since the highway was constructed. Those paths merged near the village of Ambascasas, from which the most difficult part of the climb started.

The new path was more scenic, but it was primarily mud and rocks. I wanted to walk on the highway even though it was considered more dangerous because it was shorter and I thought it would save a little energy for the final stretch. Margaret objected to that and insisted on going by the scenic route.

"Bob, you know the Spaniards are notoriously bad drivers, so it's going to be dangerous on that highway," she said.

"You can go the other way if you want," I said, "and I'll meet you at Cebrero."

Margaret wasn't giving up so easily.

"We can talk about it some more tonight," she said.

Later in the afternoon, Margaret broke out the little appetizers which we got at the restaurant and each of us had one. After that she felt like walking faster so she went on ahead. George and I met her in the evening at the refuge in Villafranca.

Villafranca is a town which grew primarily due to its position along the road to Santiago. It takes its name from the French pilgrims who had given up their goal of walking to Santiago and settled here. In the 13th century, the Spanish Pope, Calixto III granted a concession to pilgrims who were elderly and infirm. The next stage of the walk was so physically taxing that they did not have to continue on to Santiago. They were able to receive their indulgence at the church here in Villafranca.

The refuge was one of the best that we had encountered. It was relatively new and had a large dining room with a fireplace. Even Margaret gave it her stamp of approval and stayed with us.

I said, "It's a much better place than that refuge in Ponferrada, but we had one room all to ourselves so it wasn't too bad."

"Don't give me that," said Margaret. "That place in Ponferrada was awful! It was terribly cold. I saw that icebox you guys were staying in!"

We met Dominick here in Villafranca. He was a young theology student and had walked all the way from Switzerland. This was his 70th day of walking. He told me he got lost the first day after he crossed the Pyrenees and walked fifteen miles in the wrong direction. He stayed overnight with some hunters he had met. He joined us for coffee in the village and later toured the two churches with Margaret. He said he had been having a problem with his back and he was going to stay an extra day in Villafranca. That was not going to be a problem because there weren't many pilgrims on the path at this time of year.

We decided to buy some food and just have sandwiches back at the refuge rather than going out for a big meal.

After we returned to the refuge I gathered up some fire-wood which was stored on the porch and got the fireplace going while Dominick was making tea for everyone. George had bought some pomegranates for us to try. I had never eaten one before. We spread out all our food on one of the big tables and enjoyed our dinner and some good conversation around the fireplace.

The route for tomorrow remained a sticky point. Margaret and I continued to argue about which way to take. The manager of the refuge was a young woman in her thirties and she spoke excellent English. Margaret called her in to get another opinion. She asked her which way she would recommend. The manager said she would suggest going by the road although it is a bit dangerous because all you have is the river on one side and the road and the mountain on the other side. She said that, since tomorrow is Sunday, the truck traffic should be lighter. She suggested we wait until it is light, and not try to venture out in the dark. With that additional opinion Margaret agreed to go with us by the highway.

Day #30

▼

—Villafranca Del Bierzo to Cebrero, 18 Miles

George, Margaret and I shared the same room. I had already washed and was getting my boots on before Margaret and George woke up.

Margaret peered out from under her blankets and said, "Bob, do you think we could build a little fire this morning?"

"Sure, I suppose we could build a little fire. Why don't you go outside and get the wood and I'll see if I can get it started."

"Well, I didn't mean that, exactly," she said.

I laughed and said, "Oh, I know. You meant, can Bob build a fire this morning."

"Yeah, that's more like what I meant," she said.

"Okay, I'll go downstairs and see if I can get one started."

I went out on the porch and brought in some wood. It had rained during the night so the wood was wet. I tried for about twenty minutes and never could get the wood to catch fire and burn for more than a few seconds. I finally gave up.

When I came back to the room, I said, "I was only successful in burning up all the newspapers we had. Doesn't look like we'll have a fire this morning."

We had breakfast in the refuge. Last night each of us had given the manager some money and this morning she picked up fresh bakery and made coffee for us.

Before we left the refuge there was something which I really had to do.

"George, can I borrow your knife? I'm going to have to punch a hole in my belt so I can cinch it up another notch in order to keep my pants up," I said.

"Sure, I've got a blade in here which would be perfect for that," George replied.

"Bob, you do look as if you have lost quite a bit of weight," said Margaret.

"I know, and I feel good about it too. I think I have lost at least 15 pounds," I said.

Today would prove to be one of our most difficult days, ranking along with the trek from St. Jean to Roncesvalles. We planned to leave early because we didn't want to take the chance of walking the last couple of miles in the dark on the way to Cebrero. I knew if the fog came in it would be easy to get lost up there.

At seven-thirty we could see well enough to get started. It was still slightly dark so we had to be careful as we made our way through the narrow streets of the town. After going the wrong way a couple of times we finally found the small bridge that took us across the river.

Not far out of town we came to a construction site where new tunnels were being bored through the mountain. We could not determine if we should go left or right. If we went to our left we had to go through a tunnel which was 1200 feet long. The highway signs seemed to indicate that we should go right, but we thought they had been moved by the construction workers because they were bent over nearly flat on the ground. Our maps were of no use because they did not show this area very clearly.

After some discussion we decided to go left through the tunnel. Even though it was Sunday there was a lot of heavy truck traffic. At least six semi-trucks passed us as we went through the tunnel. There was just a narrow path between the wall of the tunnel and the road so we walked as close to the wall as we could and went as fast as possible to get through it.

When we came out on the other side, to our dismay, we saw some highway signs and those signs definitely told us we should have gone the other way. That meant we had to walk back through that long tunnel and put up with all those trucks again. We just hoped they could see us.

Margaret immediately started complaining and said, "Damn it! I knew we shouldn't have gone by the highway!"

"Oh, Margaret," I replied in my defense, "with all that rain last night you would be up to your armpits in mud by now if you had gone the other way."

At this point, George and I were also disgusted, not because we had taken the road, but because we had walked 2400 feet for nothing. On a day like this you did not want to take one unnecessary step.

George started lagging behind today and walking unusually slow. Margaret had been walking with him and had now moved up to walk with me for a while.

She said, "I think George is having trouble breathing. You know that city he grew up in is so polluted everyone has respiratory problems."

After talking for awhile, Margaret decided to walk faster and she moved on up ahead.

I walked a little slower until George caught up.

"How are you doing, George?" I asked.

"Oh, I'm okay," he replied.

"Are you having any trouble breathing?" I asked.

"No. Why do you ask?"

"I just wondered."

"Yesterday I was having a little pain in one leg so I wanted to take it easy for a while this morning until I could see how it was going to feel. It seems to be pretty good, so far. Did Margaret tell you we found a note from Hugo?"

"No, she didn't say anything."

"We found a page from one of those guide books under a little rock on that stone wall as we went out of town."

"I saw that, but I didn't think anything about it. What did the note say?" I asked.

"It had gotten wet from the rain and we couldn't read it," he replied.

I looked at the note and I was able to make out part of it. It appeared as if Hugo was still just one day ahead of us.

We were walking on the shoulder of highway N-VI. From time to time we had to cross construction sites because they were building a new expressway from La Corunna to Madrid. At least the construction crews were not working so that helped, but even though it was Sunday there was still a lot of truck traffic.

We stayed on the side facing the traffic which put us between the highway and the Valcarce River, with mountains all around. The river was rushing and making a lot of noise. It was so loud that sometimes it was difficult to distinguish the traffic noise from the noise of the river. It was narrow, probably only about thirty feet across at the widest point, and no more than four or five feet deep. After the rain there was a tremendous amount of water flowing down from the mountains and crashing over the big rocks.

Most of the time we were about thirty feet above the river, but the banks were loaded with trees and bushes, so there was no real danger from that side. We had no close calls on the traffic side either despite Margaret's warning that this was really stupid and dangerous.

Around noon we were approaching a small village and in the distance I could see Margaret leaving a café and starting to walk back to the trail.

I said, "Maybe Margaret's mad at us today."

George said, "No, I don't think so. I just think she's upset because her daughter is not too receptive to the idea of coming to Santiago to meet her."

"Well, it is a two-day trip from Amsterdam. Even in these modern times it's not an easy place to get to."

After about twelve miles we left the road and started the steep climb. As I walked I thought to myself, 'this is the very same trail that Sir John Moore's army took in the winter of 1809.' This steep path from Villafranca to Cebrero was of historical significance to the British Army. During the Peninsular Wars, Britain sent troops under the command of General Sir John Moore to assist the Spanish with their fight against the invading troops of Napoleon, under the command of Marshall Soult. The behavior of the English troops in Spain was barbarous and they treated the Spanish people worse than the French did. Discipline broke down as the English suffered defeats, and murder and pillage became common. Moore's army, near rebellion, finally started retreating from the French toward the port city of La Corunna.

Their most disastrous time came in January 1809, between Villafranca del Bierzo and Cebrero. It was very cold that winter and the snow was deep on this mountain pass. Many of the English wives, who had accompanied their husbands, were abandoned and left to die in the cold. The troops pushed the horses and wagons, which they no longer needed, over the cliffs into the river. They purportedly did the same with the payroll of $125,000 in gold because it was too heavy to carry.

General Moore eventually brought his rebellious troops under control, but near La Corunna, he was fatally wounded by a French cannon ball which ripped away his left arm and shoulder. Today in that city there is a statue dedicated to his memory. Six years later, on June 18, 1815, many of the men and officers of this army would go on to fight under Wellington and defeat Napoleon near the small Belgian town of Waterloo.

There was no snow on the trail today, but there were plenty of rocks and more than our share of mud. The rocks were hidden under wet leaves, which made them even more slippery and difficult to walk on. After twelve miles on the road our legs were already tired so the next six miles became torturous.

It was a difficult walk, but the scenery was beautiful. We could see small streams and green valleys below as we trudged up the path which was dark and eerie due to the large overhanging branches of the trees. At times we would be walking in ten-foot deep depressions which were only about eight feet wide. In those depressions the sides of the trail consisted of dirt, huge rocks, moss and the protruding trunks of the trees.

. George did much better walking up the hills than I did. I had to stop several times to rest and catch my breath. My right leg was beginning to hurt a lot and the arch on my right foot was aching more with every step. I tried to avoid stepping on sharp rocks with my right foot, but with leaves covering the rocks, that was impossible.

The higher we climbed the colder and foggier it became. The wind was picking up and it was beginning to get dark. We had already put on our gloves and had pulled our caps down over our ears against the cold, but the energy expended to walk made us sweat so much our shirts were wet. We were alternating between hot and cold and you could not reach a happy medium. It was a strange feeling.

One walker swiftly passed George and me. He was surely in a different league than we were. We felt good about three other walkers who were ahead of us. They were stopping frequently and we could see that they were also struggling.

"George, I can just imagine that when Luis and Christine walked this path yesterday, Christine was thinking about a divorce."

He laughed and said, "I'm sure you're right, Mister Bob. You know she was having a lot of problems with her legs and feet. She must have been dying climbing this mountain."

The sun had gone down behind the mountains and it was quickly getting dark. The wind was howling, and the fog was dense when we finally reached the top, at 4,000 feet, and walked into the desolate village of Cebrero.

"Why in the world would anyone want to live here?" George asked.

"I don't know. It is a strange looking place," I replied. "If you wanted to drop out of sight from the world, this would be the place to come."

Cebrero is believed to have Celtic origins. There are only a couple of dozen houses and buildings, and fewer than 30 inhabitants. Some of the buildings have thatched roofs and are round instead of square. During the 14th century a miracle supposedly occurred in the church here and it now stands as a sacred place to visit on the road to Santiago.

We went into the church to get our passes stamped. It was beginning to drizzle and with the fog rolling in, the village resembled a Hollywood set for a horror movie. We could now barely see where we were going. At the church we had asked the caretaker how to get to the refuge. He told us it was a stone building at the edge of the village. That wasn't a great description because they were all stone buildings, but we found it any way. It was one of those rare refuges which even had horse stalls for those few pilgrims who rode horses.

As George and I were signing the register, Margaret came in accompanied by a young couple. She introduced us to Jess, an Englishman, and to Eva, a Spanish girl.

"We have just bought some food for dinner. Jess is a chef and he's going to cook a meal for us. You two guys join us!" she said.

"Thanks anyway, but I think I'll just have something small at the restaurant. George can eat with you if he wants," I said.

I didn't think we should eat with them, especially since we didn't contribute toward the food. I know Margaret was only trying to be nice, but I didn't know how Jess and Eva would feel about it.

Jess had already walked to Santiago and was now walking back to the French border. He told us there had been a lot of rain in the last couple of days west of Cebrero and in one place he had to take off his boots and wade through water in order to get across some huge mud holes.

"George," I said, "I sure don't like the thought of wading through water."

"Maybe the water will have run off by the time we get there. The place he mentioned is still a couple of days away," George said.

There was one hostel in the village and Margaret was staying there because the refuge did not supply any blankets. We didn't know it then, but it was so hot in those rooms she probably would not have needed a blanket. Her new boots were working out well for her. Her feet and legs were holding up pretty good now so she really felt superior. I must admit she was a fast walker.

They went into the kitchen and we went to find a room. The rooms here are very small with four double bunks in each of them. The aisle between the bunks was less than two feet wide, so it was really crowded. Two people couldn't pass at the same time. The only good point about the room was that there was a heater.

The wind was still howling and I could hear a door banging someplace. It sounded as if a shutter had not been fastened and was getting caught by the wind.

When I was unpacking my bag, a young man who was staying in the room came up to me and introduced himself. His name was Matthew. He was about twenty-five years old and was from Quebec. He was very friendly, but only spoke a little English. I recognized him as the young man who had so easily passed us on the trail. He was getting ready to go to the kitchen to fix his dinner.

When George and I left the refuge to find the restaurant we had to use our flashlights to find our way in the fog. The ground was very uneven and strewn with rocks so we had to take extra care with every step. Even though the restaurant was only a couple of hundred feet from the refuge, you could not see it. It would have been easy to get lost up here on a night like this.

There were no other customers in the café so we thought they might not be serving any meals. The owner was sitting at a table reading the newspaper and watching television while his daughter, about ten years old, sat at another table and did her homework. His wife came out of the kitchen and we asked her if she could prepare dinner for us. She said she could fix noodle soup along with beefsteak and french fries. We told her that would be great.

After a while she brought us two individual bowls and then sat a huge bowl of noodle soup in the middle of the table from which we could take as much as we wanted. We were cold and hungry so each of us had two bowls of hot soup.

While we were eating our steak and fries a young married couple came in. It appeared as if they were the owner's daughter and son-in-law. The girl went behind the counter and helped herself to a coke and then she began setting one of the tables for dinner. Pretty soon she and her mother brought out a large platter of boiled potatoes, a platter of meat and a bottle of wine.

We had finished our second course and were patiently waiting for dessert. The wife interrupted her dinner to bring us our dessert which consisted of a special cheese from that area along with honey. After we finished eating we watched television because we didn't want to bother the family again in the middle of their meal. And anyway, what did we have to do? We weren't going anyplace. The Spanish feel that it is discourteous to rush you so they are rarely anxious to give you your bill and you can sit forever unless you ask for it. (I stress 'rarely' because I did find one place in Santiago where that rule did not apply).

As we left the café George got quite a scare. When he opened the door there was a German shepherd standing in the doorway wanting to come inside where it was warm. George did not argue with him. He stood to the side and the dog walked into the restaurant. We thought he may have belonged to the owners, but whether he did or not, within a few seconds after we left, the door opened and out came the dog.

When we got back to the refuge, I felt just like that dog, cold and tired. I laid down on my bunk to rest my aching legs for a while and, although I could still hear that shutter banging away somewhere in the building, it was so warm in the room I fell asleep.

I woke up about two o'clock and went to take a shower. The shutter was still making that incessant racket. When the manager was there last evening you would have thought that he would have taken a few minutes to see what that noise was, but they just don't care. I took my two money belts and passport into the bathroom with me because I noticed that Fabian was one of our roommates and I did not trust him.

DAY #31

▼

—CEBRERO TO TRIACASTELA, 14 MILES

At seven-thirty in the morning there was a knocking on our window. I saw Margaret looking in and motioning toward the door. I was wondering what the heck she was doing out there banging on the window.

George said, "The door must be locked. I'll go let her in."

Margaret came in shivering. "The weather is terrible! It's raining, it's foggy, the wind is blowing like crazy, and it's still dark."

Up until today we had really been lucky with the weather. It had not rained during the day for two or three weeks, but now it looked as if the bad weather had caught up with us.

· We went back to the restaurant where George and I had dinner last night. I ordered coffee for the three of us.

Before I could even ask the owner if he had bread and marmalade for breakfast, Margaret had taken one of their paper table cloths, spread it out over a table and was taking bread and butter out of her backpack.

"Margaret, do you think we should start eating our own food here?" I asked.

"Oh, they don't care," she said.

The owner didn't say anything, and maybe he really didn't care, but I felt bad about it so I bought six magdalenas for us and I gave him an extra tip just so he wouldn't think we were all overbearing Americans.

"Bob, how are we going to Sarria tomorrow?" Margaret asked. "You know there's a very important Benedictine Monastery in Samos which goes back to around 720 AD."

"Yes Margaret, I know that, but Samos is also four miles out of our way and that monastery has been rebuilt twice due to fires, most recently in 1951, so you'll be seeing one which is about 50 years old. It probably is nice, but I just can't see walking an extra four miles for that," I said.

"Oh, you're just in one of your anti-cultural moods today," she said. "Well, anyway, tomorrow I think I'm going by way of Samos."

Before leaving the café we had to go through the routine of getting our ponchos out and putting them on. We were bundled up and were wearing nearly all our clothes. At least that made the backpack a little lighter.

It was a terrible morning to be walking. Margaret soon walked off and left George and me. The wind was blowing fiercely and it was raining steadily. The path at first lead through heather which was as high as our heads. It was easy to take the wrong path if you were not watchful for the yellow arrows. We could only see about thirty feet in front of us.

Eventually George and I did take the wrong path. We were near some farms and we took one of the paths out into the fields. The path consisted of large rocks and most of the time you could use them for stepping stones, but that was like playing hopscotch. Eventually you stepped in mud about four inches deep, and sometimes it wasn't just mud, it was also cow manure. They also ran their cows down this path. We lost more than half an hour walking in this mud before we realized we were going the wrong way. We finally backtracked and got on the path again.

At noon the wind and rain had still not let up. We had been walking in it for four hours through mud and manure and up and down extremely steep hills, and we were being buffeted in every direction by the strong wind. The hills were so steep and slippery I had to use my staff to keep my balance while climbing up them. With the poncho on I was wet with sweat, my glasses were so fogged up I could not see where I was going, and I was totally out of breath. I finally told George that I had to take a rest. We saw some big rocks and we staggered up to them and plopped down, exhausted. My spirits were pretty low because I was out of breath and it seemed as if the rain and blowing wind was never going to stop.

I said, "George, I don't know about you, but I can't take any more of this mud and these hills. When we get back to the highway again, I'm going to take it to Triacastela. If you want to continue on the path, go ahead and I'll meet you at the refuge."

"I've had it too," George said, as he wiped his glasses, "I can't see a damned thing!"

As we were sitting on the rocks resting, I looked up the next hill as the fog was lifting a little. "Look, there's some kind of building up there," I said. "I can barely see the outline of a roof through the fog."

We struggled up the steep muddy hill and found a café at the top. It was Alto del Poio, one of the highest points on the walk, so if we walked on the road it should all be down hill from here. I had been thinking so much about the difficult stretch between Villafranca and Cebrero that I had convinced myself the rest of the way would be easy. Maybe it was a big mistake to think there were going to be any easy days ahead of us.

We went into the café, took off our wet ponchos and backpacks and put them on the floor.

The lady who owned the place welcomed us, saying, "Come in. Come in. You must be cold."

There was a fireplace, but no fire was going. It was also cold in the café, you could even see your breath, but it was not as bad as outside. It was too bad Margaret was not along. She would have asked the owner if we could build a fire. George and I had hot chocolate and a couple of magdalenas and rested for about half an hour. The wind was so strong it kept blowing the door open and we finally put a chair against it to keep it shut.

The lady who owned the café told us it was eight miles to Triacastela. That meant we had only covered six miles in the last four hours, but under those conditions I guess that wasn't too bad, especially since we lost some time by taking the wrong path.

There was not much traffic on the road, and even with the fog it wasn't too dangerous. We watched the oncoming traffic closely to make sure they weren't swerving toward us on the shoulder. I'm sure it was hard for the drivers to see us. I walked in front because I had a bright yellow poncho and a driver would see that much sooner than he would see George's dark green one.

When we reached the refuge at Triacastela, the manager gave us a note from Margaret. She had checked into the local hostel.

We walked into the main part of the village to the pharmacy. George's leg was aching and he wanted to see if he could buy something for it.

We looked for the hostel, but apparently we didn't walk far enough to see it. We went back to the café which was near the refuge to have a drink. It was now about five o'clock and it was that in between time when cafes did not fix hot meals. We wanted to have an omelette sandwich which was considered a hot meal so that was out. We settled for cheese instead. The sandwich was so big I told George I was going to consider that my lunch and dinner.

In the evening Margaret came over to the refuge and admonished us for not coming to the hostel to look her up. George kept her happy by telling her he would have dinner with her. I decided not to go to dinner because I had that big sandwich. I said I was going back to the café and have something small and spend the evening getting my journal up to date.

Margaret said she was going to Samos tomorrow and did not know if she would make it to Sarria or not. That was where George and I had planned to stay so if she did not get there we might not see her again. We exchanged e-mail addresses just in case she did not make it.

After George and Margaret left I sat at the manager's desk reading the registration book to see what countries had been represented by pilgrims in the last few months. I was surprised to see that within the last couple of months there had been two pilgrims from Russia and two from Poland, as well as a few from Japan. While I was looking at the book, Matthew came along.

"Did you have dinner?" he asked.

"No, but I had a big sandwich earlier, so I'm not hungry," I replied.

"I have plenty of food. I'll fix you something to eat if you want. You can eat with me," Matthew said.

"Oh no, that's okay. It's just that I'm not hungry. I had a big cheese sandwich about five o'clock, so that was enough," I said, "but thanks a lot anyway."

After Matthew left I went across to the café and sat there for a couple of hours drinking coffee, watching the news on television and updating my journal.

Day #32

▼

—Triacastela to Sarria, 11 Miles

We had breakfast at the café near the refuge and began walking about eight-thirty. The weather was slightly over-cast, but it was not cold and it was not raining. We had originally intended to walk to Barbadelo which is three miles past Sarria, but there is nothing in Barbadelo, not even a place to eat. We decided to stop in Sarria instead which is a town with a population of about 15,000. We also thought it would be the best place to meet up with Margaret again if she made it that far.

The walk today was scenic and enjoyable. We had stopped to determine how we were going to get through a path which was mostly submerged by running water when Eva caught up with us.

We had first met her at Cebrero. She was a very nice girl, twenty-eight years old, from Gijon, which is near Barcelona. She started walking in Villafranca and she was only going to walk for a week. She had two weeks vacation from her job, but she was going back home to help her father in his business for a week.

We also met two middle-aged Spanish couples. We were resting on some rocks when they approached us. One of the husbands and the two wives were walking ahead and the other husband was walking a couple of hundred yards behind. They stopped and talked with us for a while. They had just started walking today. When we told them this was our 32nd day, they were really impressed, and it made us feel like veterans.

As we talked it started to rain a little and the husband who was lagging behind started to put on his poncho. His wife, an attractive red-headed woman, attempted to help him, but he angrily told her he could do it himself. She replied that she was just trying to help. We could sense that there was a little friction between them. She spoke English without a trace of an accent and when I first talked to her I thought she might be from Britain, but I later found out she was Spanish.

It was obvious that the wives had gone shopping before taking this trip. They were dressed as if they had just walked out of an expensive sporting goods store. One woman was outfitted in bright red clothes while the red-headed woman was wearing a very nice bright yellow jacket and bright yellow boots. I was wondering what those pretty boots would look like when they got to Santiago, if they got there at all.

We arrived in Sarria around four o'clock. We were the first ones to check in at the refuge so we had our pick of the beds. We went upstairs to a room which faced the street. It had several French doors which opened onto a tiny balcony. I took a bed near the doors and George took the one next to me.

As we were spreading out our things we heard voices downstairs. George went down to see who it was. I could hear George and someone else talking as they came back up the stairs. I thought the voice was familiar. It was Hugo.

He said that when he got into El Acebo another pilgrim showed up who told him we were going to go on to Ponferrada, so he decided to push on also. He said he walked over twenty miles that day and his legs and feet were killing him with pain. After it got dark he tried to catch a ride by hitchhiking, but no one would stop. He said he couldn't blame them, he probably wouldn't have stopped either.

Hugo had stayed here in Sarria last night and he asked Feena, the manager, if he could stay another night because a friend of his, Bouke, was driving to Sarria from Amsterdam to meet him. Feena said it was against the rules, but she would allow it because they had plenty of empty beds. Hugo then struck a deal with her, for a price, to store Bouke's car in a garage there. The garage belonged to Feena's friend.

We were really glad to see Hugo again. He had a good sense of humor and was good company, and we had not heard the *Rawhide* song in days. It was also obvious that he was genuinely glad to see us again.

It was getting late to have lunch, so we asked Feena where we could go for something to eat. She gave us the name of a small place about a block away and said, "Tell them Feena sent you."

"What did she mean by that?" Hugo asked.

"Maybe we'll get served if we tell them that, because it's getting awfully late for lunch," I said.

It was a family restaurant with only six tables. The people at one table were finishing their lunch and getting ready to leave. No other tables were occupied. We were just getting in at the last minute.

An older lady was waiting on the tables and also making the food, while her husband served customers at the bar. She did not say anything, but it appeared that she was not elated to see us come in at that time for lunch. A young woman was sitting at one of the front tables feeding a small baby. I assumed this was the daughter and grandchild of the owners. Presently a young man, probably the son-in-law, came in, picked up a huge loaf of bread and started tearing it apart as he sat down with the daughter and baby. After our food was served, the grandmother brought out food and sat down with the young couple. The grandfather opened a bottle of wine and joined them for lunch.

We ate slowly and talked because we knew it was going to be a long time before we got any more attention. This gave us a chance to hear of Hugo's adventures over the last few days.

Hugo spoke pretty good Spanish, but he was having trouble here. He said, "George, I'm having a hard time understanding these people."

"I know what you mean. They are either speaking Gallegan, or some other Spanish dialect, and even though Gallegan is supposed to be close to Portuguese, it is also hard for me to understand," George replied.

Hugo continued, "I went to Lugo for the day and I was going to take the train. At the train station this morning I asked the man at the window what time the train left for Lugo. I understood him to say eight-nineteen and since I had plenty of time, I sat down and had a cup of coffee. In a few minutes I saw a train stop and leave, and I was thinking that it looked like such a nice train. I didn't know it then, but that was my train! He had said nineteen minutes before eight, not nineteen minutes after eight. I ended up taking the bus instead."

As we were finishing our wine, George picked up the bottle and said, "Look at this. It's red wine, but the label says '*blanco*.'"

Hugo laughed and said, "They must refill the bottles and use them again."

When we got back to the refuge we found that Margaret had arrived. She had recognized our backpacks and had taken a bunk in the same room that we were occupying. She had gone by way of Samos and, just for my information, the monastery was absolutely fantastic and was well worth walking the extra distance.

Hugo called his friend Bouke on his cell phone. Bouke was on the road and was about twenty miles from Sarria. Hugo told him he had arranged for a garage and that he would save a bunk for him in our room.

When Bouke arrived, Hugo introduced him to us. We liked him instantly. He was tall, in his fifties, with bushy graying hair and a gray mustache. Feena prepared a pilgrim's pass for him and he said he was going to walk with us to Santiago. He and Hugo then planned to take a bus back from there to pick up the car.

We stayed around the refuge for the rest of the evening, and took care of some necessities, such as taking showers, and washing socks.

That evening we went to a slightly upscale restaurant for dinner, much better than what George and I would have chosen.

While we were eating, three of the people from the two Spanish couples came in for dinner. The red-headed woman was not with them. Of course, George and I had to tell our walking companions what we had observed during the day. It seemed as if there was some conflict going on among them. It was unfortunate that our lives had been reduced to this. With nothing else to occupy our minds we observed everyone else and took an interest in what they were doing.

It was getting late when we finally finished dinner. We had to walk quickly to get back to the refuge before the door was locked.

Day #33

▼

—Sarria to Portomarin, 16 Miles

When we woke up, Hugo said, "What a night! We had a lot of drama going on, in addition to all the snoring."

I must have slept pretty soundly, because I did not know anything about last night, so I asked, "What happened?"

They related the story to me.

About midnight, Margaret said, "George, wake up. There's someone tapping on the glass."

"That can't be," he said, "we're on the second floor."

The tapping then grew louder.

"Well, I don't care, I know there's someone out there," she said.

The person tapping on the window probably thought no one was going to get up and let him in so he pushed the French doors open and came inside.

As he walked through the room, he looked at George and said, "Excuse me."

He headed on down to the other room. The front door had been locked at ten-thirty and apparently he had stayed out too late eating dinner and drinking, and had gotten locked out.

When we left the refuge that morning we took a closer look at our balcony. We figured our intruder had probably climbed up on a garbage can and then pulled himself up to the balcony.

There was a coffee shop just across the street from the refuge. All of us met there to have coffee and breakfast. While we were there half a dozen of the ever-present policemen from the Guardia Civil came in for their morning coffee.

The weather alternated between sun and rain, but for the most part it was an enjoyable day of walking. The path through the countryside was filled with rocks and water. It was challenging, but interesting and fun, especially since we did not have to do any wading.

We also had some good company with Hugo and Bouke along. Bouke was much more reserved than Hugo. Occasionally Hugo would break out with a song. In addition to the theme from *Rawhide* he liked a number of old rock and roll songs. He could always expect to be accompanied when Margaret was along.

Our destination today was Portomarin. Matthew had told us he was going to Gonzar which was about four miles farther on. That would make twenty miles for him today, but if anyone could do it, it would be Matthew. He was a strong and fast walker.

He wanted to be in a small village where it would be very dark because it was November 17th and this was the night that the earth would pass through the wake of the Tempel-Tuttle comet, which circles the sun once every 33 years. He wanted to be able to see the resulting meteor shower which could only be seen in this hemisphere. It probably was dark enough in Portomarin, but later that evening I forgot all about it.

As we walked today we met Lola and Gonsalvo. They were both in their twenties. She was from Mexico and he was from Spain. From what we could determine it looked as if he were carrying some of her things as well as his own.

"He looks like a strong boy," George said, "so she has loaded him down with her stuff too."

"That reminds me of the old days," Margaret said, "when men were men and not wimps."

"What are 'wimps'?" George asked. "That's not another name for 'George' is it?"

Margaret ignored George's comment and continued, "When my husband and I used to take our kids for hikes in the California mountains, we used to carry a lot more than this. Sometimes we would kill a deer and cook it at a campfire."

Margaret continued telling us about her camping trips as we plodded along toward the Mino River. Between 1956 and 1963 the Spanish government built a huge reservoir by damming the river. The original town of Portomarin was completely covered with water. They dismantled the Church of Saint Nicolas, stone by stone, and moved it about a mile from the original site and reassembled it. The government also built houses for the inhabitants and businesses and moved them as well.

As we came out of the hills I could see the new town gleaming white across the river. To get there it was necessary to walk over a very long and high bridge. Just walking across this bridge high above the water was exciting. I had been told that when the water was low you could see some of the old structures, but today, even from this vantage point, I could not see any of the remains of the old town.

The refuge was a one-story building. There was no heat, but there was hot water. Neither of the stoves in the kitchen worked.

Margaret wanted to see the church, but it was only open when there was a mass. She asked us to go along so Bouke, Hugo and I accompanied her.

During the mass I looked at the stones carefully. They were all very clean and neat and the church did not have the appearance of a building which had been standing for a couple of hundred years.

At dinner we had a good chance to talk to Bouke and learn a little more about him. He was married and had three sons. His wife's name was Arjon. His last name was Jaron, so that made her name Arjon Jaron, an anagram. They named their first son, Casper. Later they realized all their initials together were ABC, so when they had twin boys three years later they named them Dorian and Ewald to keep the alphabet going.

Bouke and his wife had also travelled a lot. His wife had worked for the Dutch government for a long time when she was sent to the island of St. Maarten as an auditor. Bouke and the boys accompanied her. While they were living there Bouke started a sailing school and they also built a home on the island. They now rent the home to vacationers for additional income.

George did not go to dinner with us tonight. I believe that George liked Eva a lot. He had been talking to her quite a bit and she invited him to have drinks with her and Luis, Augusto and Baltasar, the Spanish guys with whom she had been walking. They were old guys and they had taken a fatherly attitude toward Eva. She said they were always trying to fix her up with an eligible bachelor. Eva and George were not drinkers, but the other three liked to have a drink or two, or three after dinner. We were teasing George and told him he was falling in with bad company.

We had returned to the refuge and were getting ready for bed when Bouke received a call from his wife. She was calling to tell him that a category 5 hurricane, which was the most powerful, was moving toward St. Maarten.

Hugo told us that he and Bouke might have to return to Amsterdam tomorrow.

Day #34

▼

—Portomarin to Palas De Rei, 16 Miles

"Wow! Did I sleep good last night!" Margaret said as she got up.

"You sure did sleep good," George said. "You were really snoring."

"Oh, come on!" she said.

"He's right, Margaret," Hugo agreed. "I had to get up in the middle of the night and move your bunk away from the wall. It was rattling so hard it was keeping everyone awake."

"Geez! I get one decent night's sleep out of thirty nights with you guys," she laughed, "and I have to take this kind of ribbing!"

Before we prepared to leave that morning, Bouke phoned home to see if he could get some news about conditions in St. Maarten. He was sitting in the kitchen speaking to his wife while Hugo, Margaret and I stood in the hallway outside the door. They were speaking Dutch so Hugo had to tell us what was going on.

He said, "From the look on his face and what he's saying, it does not sound very good. We'll just have to wait until he gets off the phone."

After finishing his call Bouke came out and, visibly distressed, said, "It does not look good. The storm is not moving much. It is now just hammering the island. I guess the house could be a total loss, unless we're lucky. It's impossible to contact anyone on the island so my wife has not been able to talk to the people who are staying there."

Hugo said, "What do you want to do? If you want to go back and get the car and head home, I'll go with you."

"Well, there's absolutely nothing I can do whether I'm here or at home. All the flights into St. Maarten have been cancelled. So we might as well keep walking. Maybe that will take my mind away from it," he said.

As we were walking out of Portomarin I met a young English girl, to whom I'd spoken the evening before. She did not have her backpack.

"Hi, where's your backpack?" I asked.

"The three Spanish guys and I hired a taxi to take our bags to Melide," she replied.

I was teasing her when I said, "Now, is the Pope going to think that's kosher?"

She had started in Le Puy, France and with a big smile she said, "After walking for 56 days, I don't give a damn whether it's kosher or not. It feels great to walk without carrying something."

"It's twenty five miles to Melide, so it's still going to be a tough day for you," I said.

"I know it is," she said, "but my father is coming down to Santiago on Saturday so I have to get there by then."

I wished her good luck and then she went on her way.

After traversing a high narrow footbridge over the river we were back on the path again. The walk to Palas de Rei was not bad, but George said he was not feeling in tip-top shape. His head hurt a little and his stomach was upset. He said maybe he had too much to drink last night.

The refuge in Palas de Rei was on the main street in town and it was a pretty good place. Margaret was not able to get any blankets, so she decided to get a room in the hostel next door.

After checking into the refuge, George and I went to a café at another hostel up the street to have coffee. When we entered we saw the two middle-aged Spanish couples. At one table one of the husbands and the two wives were having bacon and eggs for their lunch, and at another table the red-headed woman's husband was sitting alone having bacon and eggs. I guess they were still fighting.

Later that evening we had dinner in the restaurant at this same hostel. George did not go with us. While we were eating he came in with Eva, Luis, Augusto and Baltasar. He came over to our table for a minute and we told him not to have too much to drink after dinner.

He said, "I'll try not to have too much, but you know they really do like to drink. And they drink that clear liquor. I don't know the name of it, but it's pretty powerful."

Day #35

▼

—Palas De Rei to Ribadiso De Baixo, 17 Miles

We had decided to double up again today and go for seventeen miles. My feet and legs were holding up just fine. Bouke had a blister, but he thought he would be able to walk that distance.

Margaret had convinced her daughter, Jill to come to Santiago. So she was going to walk as far as Melide with us and then take a bus the rest of the way. Lola and Gonsalvo had joined us on the walk today.

A few miles before we got to Melide we had stopped in a café for coffee. The woman who owned the café told us her son owned a restaurant in Melide and she gave Lola her card with a note. She told us that if we gave her son the card he would give us free coffee if we had lunch there.

Melide is a town of about 10,000 population. We found the bus station and checked to see what time the next bus was leaving. There was plenty of time for Margaret to have lunch with us.

We were nearly out of town when we found the restaurant at the western most part of the main street. It was a large restaurant, probably with at least forty tables.

After we had our lunch Lola gave the card to the young waiter and he said it was just good for one coffee. She told him that she wanted to see the manager. The manager came over, and after looking at the card, told her we could all have free coffee.

Margaret walked back to the bus station. We agreed to meet at the cathedral in Santiago on Sunday at six o'clock in the evening.

According to the guide books which we had there was no place to get anything to eat in Ribadiso. On the way out of town George and I stopped at a small grocery store and bought ham and cheese. A short distance further on we stopped at a bakery and bought a big loaf of bread, which was in the shape of a circle. It looked like a wheel. We already had some grapes and oranges. That was going to be our dinner tonight.

The path from Melide to Ribadiso was through forests and fields which made the walk very pleasant and scenic. The fields were still green in Galicia and even at this time of year most of the trees still had their leaves. Rainfall in this area is abundant and all the streams were filled with water, and sometimes even the path was filled with water. Fortunately there were usually big stones strewn about which could be used as steps to get through these low lying areas without getting wet.

Just a couple of hundred yards before we reached the refuge we saw a café. We stopped in and had a hot chocolate. There was a big fireplace loaded with logs fully ablaze. A young boy sat at a table before the fire doing his school homework.

George talked to the woman who appeared to be the owner. He told her the books which we had did not indicate that there was a café near the refuge in Ribadiso. She said they had just opened in May.

The refuge was a newer place and overall a nice one. The design, however, was not perfect. In order to get to the kitchen, which was in another building, it was necessary to go outside. And you had to go outside to yet another building to get to the showers and toilets. Going to the washroom in the middle of the night was a lot of fun, especially since it was real cold that night.

They also made extensive use of Dutch doors in this refuge. I think they probably did that in order to be able to open the upper part for fresh air while keeping the lower part closed to prevent the mice from coming in. There were a lot of field mice in the area. The doors invariably did not fit perfectly and when you tried to open them they made a horrible scraping sound against the stone floor. It was impossible to open them quietly in the middle of the night.

Eva and her friends asked us to eat dinner with them that evening. Augustino and Luis had gone to the local hostel and talked the owner into making some omelettes for us.

We met all of them in the kitchen at 8:00 that evening. In addition to myself there was George, Bouke, Hugo, Eva, Luis, Augustino, Gonsalvo and Lola.

We brought our big loaf of bread, along with the ham, cheese, grapes, oranges and candy. They brought two frying pans from the hostel, each containing a huge omelette the size of a big pie. They cut the omelettes and passed them around. Eva had brought some of that same cheese which I had in Cebrero. They had also acquired three bottles of wine and one bottle of that clear liquor which reminded me of moonshine. After the wine was finished the liquor was passed around as an after dinner drink. As George had said, it was powerful stuff. I could only take a small drink.

We thought we could leave our food on the table overnight without the mice getting to it and we would have some ham and cheese in the morning for breakfast.

George was kidding the Spaniards about getting a late start every day and said, "We'll have to have two breakfast times, one for us at eight o'clock and one for Eva and her friends at nine o'clock."

Eva laughed and said, "I just love it when I hear you guys getting ready in the morning because then I know I still have another hour to sleep."

Day #36

▼

—Ribadiso De Baixo to Santa Irene, 14 Miles

We did not have breakfast in the refuge. We decided to walk to Arzua which was a fairly good size town three miles away.

It was cold that morning. There was frost on the grass, but the air was clear and fresh. There was a nice view of the surrounding hills and a green valley with trees and grass glistening with frost, and in the distance smoke was rising from the chimneys of the farm houses. It was a pleasant view.

In Arzua we found a good place to eat. At breakfast it was just George, Hugo, Bouke and me.

As we were eating, Hugo said, "Well guys, did anyone ever find out how old Margaret is?"

"No, we never did," I said. "But I did get a good clue yesterday. She told me her son is 37 years old."

"I think she has to be close to 60," George said.

"She sure doesn't look like it," said Hugo, "but I guess that would have to be about right."

Hugo and Bouke had told us they were going to walk to Santa Irene and then go back and get the car. They were going to drive into Santiago tomorrow for the pilgrim's mass at noon and then leave right away and head for Chartres, France, to pick up Hugo's bicycle and then continue on to Amsterdam. A total journey of about 1,200 miles.

Just before we were leaving Eva and her friends came into the restaurant. After we exchanged greetings, Eva told us that last night a mouse had gotten into her backpack and tore open her packs of sugar.

She said, "When I heard paper rustling in the night, I thought it was Augustino and I was wondering 'what is he doing?'"

Augustino said he thought it was Eva rustling paper.

Bouke said, "I knew there were mice in there last night. I heard them trying to get into my backpack so I got out of bed and moved it to an upper bunk which wasn't being used. Then they went over and were trying to get into Hugo's pack." All of us had a good laugh about this.

I treated Hugo, Bouke and George to breakfast that morning. I told them it was just to show them my appreciation for their good company.

Hugo and Bouke walked on ahead of us because they wanted to get to Santa Irene early enough to catch a bus and go back to Sarria for the car.

Late in the afternoon my right foot started to hurt. I was limping along for about an hour when we came to a restaurant. George and I went in to have lunch.

Eva, Luis, Augustino and Baltasar were already there eating. They said they had decided to go on to Lavacolla which was a few miles further. That would make it possible for them to get to Santiago in time for the pilgrim's mass at noon.

While we were eating, the waitress brought over two glasses of wine for us, compliments of Eva and her friends. They were having their after dinner drinks and were just about to depart. We did not think we would see them again.

"George, I think you really like Eva," I said.

"Yeah, I do. She is something special. It's too bad she lives on the wrong continent," he said.

During our lunch I took my right boot off to ease the pressure on my aching foot. When we left the restaurant my foot was feeling pretty good. I think I could have gone a few more miles, but Santa Irene was less than a mile away.

The refuge was on the main highway. It was a new two-story place and the room which we selected had six double bunks and plenty of heat. There was a heater on the wall under the window and it was turned up to the maximum. After washing my socks I hung them on a chair near the heater and, within half an hour, they were dry.

George and I were the only ones in the refuge. The manager was a young woman in her twenties. While I was taking a shower George sat at the receptionist's table and talked to her.

She had been the manager since the beginning of the year. She said her one-year contract was going to be up soon and she was definitely not going to renew it. She said she was unbelievably busy during the summer because there were so many pilgrims and because of the crowding there were a lot of arguments and problems. She had become tired of that and was going to try to find another job.

George asked her what kind of jobs were available around there. She readily admitted that there wasn't much to do. Her husband had a construction job and he was working pretty steadily. She said a lot of the women worked on the farms tending to the cows and sheep. In Galicia we had noticed that nearly all the people tending herds of cows were women.

About seven o'clock the manager's husband came by to pick her up. She gave the keys to George and said that we were in charge.

"Just put the keys on the table when you leave in the morning," she said.

Within the next hour, while we were in charge, we had just a few customers. A group of four pilgrims arrived just to get their passes stamped. They were continuing on to Arzua. There was an Englishwoman among them.

She said to me, "Mud and manure, that's what it is! It should be called the M & M camino."

I was lying on my bunk trying to read a Spanish newspaper when the front door opened and a young man came in with several passes. He wanted to stamp them and I showed him where the stamp was kept. I watched as he stamped ten passes, three times each. I followed him when he left and I saw two vans with about ten people inside. I thought they were probably tourists who wanted to have passes which looked genuine. I was wondering if they were going to try to get *compostelas* with those passes when they reached Santiago.

"George, do you want to walk back up to that restaurant and have coffee and maybe a bowl of soup?" I asked.

"Sure, whenever you're ready," he replied, "but I think we may have to walk on the road rather than the path. It would be too dark going through the woods."

"That'll be okay. It's only about half a mile," I said, "and there's a full moon tonight. I'll write a note and leave it on the door in case Hugo and Bouke return while we are gone."

We bundled up, locked the front door and started off. We had only been gone about five minutes when we reached the place where the path leaves the road and goes into the forest.

We could see a light coming out of the woods and we heard voices. It was a young Brazilian girl, Margot, and a Portuguese fellow, Aldo. They were headed for the Santa Irene refuge. We told them the manager had gone home, but that we had the keys. We gave them the keys and told them we would be back in a while.

George did not have a good impression of Aldo. As we continued on to the restaurant, he said, "Do you have your valuables with you Mister Bob?"

"I have everything with me," I replied. "If they go through my backpack, they won't find anything except dirty clothes."

Two young girls, sitting at the bar, were the only people in the restaurant, and they appeared to be family members. We sat down there too and George asked the waitress what they had to eat. We didn't want a full dinner, but maybe just a bowl of soup.

She said they did not have the soup ready yet, but they did have another dish which they could serve. She described the dish to George.

"I'm not exactly sure what she means, but I think it's some kind of dish made with pig's feet and beans," he told me.

"I think I can do without that. Maybe I'll just have a croissant and coffee," I said.

Just at that moment all the lights went out. We were in total darkness until they could get some candles lit and positioned on the bar.

George and I stayed there about an hour drinking coffee and eating croissants. The lights never did come back on.

When we were walking back to the refuge we met Aldo and Margot headed for the restaurant. We told them the lights had gone out. They said the lights had not gone out in the refuge. They decided to continue on, hoping that by the time they got to the restaurant the lights would have come on again.

After we got back to the refuge we went around and closed all the windows, which we had not thought about before we left. While we were doing that the front door bell rang.

It was Hugo and Bouke. They had returned from Sarria with Bouke's car, a Peugeot station wagon. Bouke still did not have any more news about the storm in St. Maarten.

Aldo and Margot had taken bunks in the room which we occupied. There were six bunks in that room. Hugo and Bouke didn't want to be too crowded, so they decided to take bunks in the large dormitory upstairs.

They asked us if we wanted to go someplace to get something to eat. We told them we had just come back from the restaurant and since we had the keys we felt an obligation to stay there because Aldo and Margot would be returning pretty soon.

When Aldo and Margot returned they told us the electricity had been restored at the cafe and they were able to get something to eat. Aldo and I chatted while George was having a conversation with Margot, a fellow Brazilian. Aldo was a bassist studio musician in Madrid. He was half Spanish and half Portuguese. He had spent 2 years in California when he was very young so his English was excellent.

DAY #37

▼

—SANTA IRENE TO SANTIAGO—
13 MILES

This was the day we had been looking forward to. It was the final day in our long journey.

As Hugo and I were sitting at the receptionist's table putting on our boots, he said, "Bob, we're going to stop at a little restaurant only a couple of miles up the road, but I just know it's no use offering you guys a ride."

"No. We really appreciate it though, but you understand that we have walked every step of the way up to this point so we just can't take a ride," I said.

"I knew that's what you would say. If I were in your place, I would say the same thing."

We said our farewells to Hugo and Bouke. We really hated to see them go. They were nice people and had been good friends and good company along the road.

We followed them outside and watched as they put their backpacks in the station wagon. We waved goodbye as they drove away. Very shortly they would be in Santiago and after the mass they were driving on to Bilbao.

We walked to the restaurant which Hugo had mentioned. When we ordered our coffee, the woman asked if we wanted it to be half coffee and half milk or if we preferred a greater amount of coffee than milk.

George was astonished. He said to the waitress, "That is good service. No one has ever asked us that before. I really appreciate that you want to serve your customers well."

"This is my business," she said, "and the better I treat my customers, the more customers I have."

George turned to me and said, "Wow. At least someone in Spain is finally understanding the meaning of service."

This was not because we had received poor service in Spain. On the whole the service had always been good, but it had always been a little laid back.

Cebrero was supposedly 160 kilometers from Santiago. At that point we began to see stone markers every one-half kilometer counting down the distance to Santiago. The last marker we saw said 12 kilometers, which would be about 7.2 miles.

We walked and walked and finally I said, "I wonder why we aren't seeing any more distance markers."

George said, "I'll bet after they got to this point they realized they had miscalculated so they just stopped putting up the markers."

I found that hard to believe, but for whatever reason, we never saw another marker. We did, however, see a couple of memorials to pilgrims who had died on the way to Santiago. There seemed to be more in Galicia than on other sections of the camino, but that was probably due to the fact that many people started their journey in Cebrero.

One of the memorials was dedicated to a 69-year-old priest who had died while making the pilgrimage in 1993. His hiking boots were encased in cement in the memorial and there was a small plaque describing his life.

It was pleasant walking today as we wandered through forests of tall eucalyptus trees. There was a pleasant scent in the fresh air. A great number of trees had been cut and were stacked up waiting for the lumber truck. Today was Sunday so there would not be any coming today. The only other local people we saw were hunters who were out early this morning.

As we neared the airport we could hear the roar of jet engines as the planes sat at the end of the runway. We walked near a tall fence which kept people from wandering onto the runways.

Shortly we came to the top of one of the many hills and could see Santiago there before us. It was still quite a distance to the city. We continued to follow the yellow arrows and they lead us through the outskirts of the town and through the ancient streets to the cathedral. It was 3:30 in the afternoon on Sunday, November 21st when we entered the cathedral, after walking for 37 straight days.

The cathedral was crowded with tourists. We saw Lola and Gonsalvo right away after we entered. They had arrived the day before. She looked well rested, but Gonsalvo looked tired.

We went from the cathedral directly to the pilgrim's office, which was only a couple of doors away. There a young woman examined our passes and questioned us about the origin of our journey and asked if we had

walked all the way. She then prepared our *compostelas,*
which is the official document certifying that you have
completed the requirements for the indulgence.

She asked us if we would be attending the mass at noon
tomorrow and we said that we would. She said the archbishop would announce that there were two pilgrims in
attendance who had walked from St. John Pied de Port.

While we were in the pilgrim's office, our friend,
Dominick, whom we had met in Villafranca came in.
He had just arrived in Santiago. He said tomorrow he
was going to continue on to Finisterre, which was about
sixty miles away on the Atlantic, but he said he might go
by bus.

I suspected that Margaret and Jill might be staying at
Hostel Suso, because Margaret and I had talked about
that hotel. We walked over there to see about a room, but
there was a note on the door saying they had no vacan-
cies. I had the name of another place, the Hospedaje
Santa Cruz, just a few doors away at 42 Rua do Vilar. The
hotel is on the second floor and after climbing the stairs I
found a note on the door saying to inquire at 80 Rua do
Vilar for rooms.

There was a small fruit store at that address. I asked the
woman behind the counter about rooms. Right away she
took George and me back to the hotel and showed us a
double room. It was very clean with two single beds. The
steeple of the cathedral was visible from the bedroom window. Down the hall there was a big washroom with
shower and bath. The cost was $21 per night. We agreed
that it was fine and paid the woman for two nights. She
gave us three keys, one to the street door, one to the door

on the second floor and one to our room. We never saw her after that.

The room was small, but everything was clean and the location of the hotel was ideal. It was just 3 or 4 minutes walk to the cathedral and this was one of the busy streets in the city. It was more like a pedestrian mall rather than a street. The only vehicles which were allowed on the street were delivery trucks. There were a lot of souvenir and coffee shops in this area.

George and I decided to go out and do a little window shopping. As we were looking in a souvenir shop window, someone grabbed my arm. It was Margaret. She was with her daughter, Jill.

Jill said, "I told my mother I saw two men who looked like Bob and George. She had described you two so well that I thought I would recognize you anywhere."

It was nice to finally meet Jill. She was very friendly and talkative and both George and I liked her right away. She had taken the train from Amsterdam on Thursday and arrived in Santiago on Saturday.

They asked us where we were staying. I told them we were staying just a few doors away and that we first tried Hostel Suso, but it was filled up. We took them to our hotel and showed them our room. They said they were staying at Hostel Suso and they were paying a lot more for their room and it wasn't that much better. We had dinner with them that evening and agreed to meet them for coffee the next morning.

SANTIAGO—MONDAY, NOVEMBER 22, 1999

▼

I got up around six-thirty and it really felt good to know I didn't have to walk a few miles today. I went out just before eight o'clock and I told George I would meet him downstairs at eight-thirty.

I had seen a coffee shop just a couple of doors away from our hotel so I went there and had a cup of coffee. I took a table near the window and watched the people passing by on the sidewalk. Some were carrying books and were obviously students on their way to class. Many of the others were on their way to work while some were carrying backpacks and I suspected they were on their way to the train station.

At nine o'clock we met Margaret and Jill at the Hotel Suso coffee shop, which was across the street and a few doors to the right from our hotel.

After breakfast Jill went back to the room while Margaret walked down to the train station with George and me.

I needed to get a seat reservation on the train to San Sebastian tomorrow. In Spain, even if you already have a ticket for a train you must also get a seat reservation. The train was scheduled to leave Santiago at nine o'clock in the morning and arrive in San Sebastian at eight o'clock that evening.

Margaret wanted George to help her talk to the man at the information desk. She had all kinds of questions about trains going to Portugal, but she wasn't exactly sure where she wanted to go.

On the way back from the station, she saw a sign in a travel agent's window advertising a cheap rate for a seven-day vacation in the Canary Islands. She and George went in to get the details. Of course, they didn't have any tickets left for the super-cheap package, but they did have some which were a little more costly. Margaret suspected this to be a "bait and switch" deal and said she would talk it over with Jill.

We headed back to the center of town.

Margaret said, "I'm going back to the hotel to talk to Jill. Maybe we can decide where we want to go."

"George and I are going over by the cathedral. Maybe we'll see some people coming into town that we know," I said.

"You've got to be kidding," Margaret laughed. "You guys never did pass anyone. Who could be coming into town that you know? Everyone you know has been here for a couple of days."

The main goal of every pilgrim is to reach the magnificent church in Santiago. It is known as the Cathedral of the Apostle and it was constructed between 1075 and 1211. The crypt in its lower level is said to contain the remains of Saint James. It is a huge Romanesque edifice with a lavish baroque facade. The eastern door, the *Portico de la Gloria*, is the first part of the building which pilgrims see when approaching the cathedral. This door is only open during the Holy Years.

The cathedral looks much more lavish from the *Plaza do Obradoiro*, which is on the west side of the building. This huge plaza affords you an opportunity to stand far back from this grand building and take in all its beauty.

There are two other large buildings facing this plaza. One is the city hall, which is in an elegant 18th century building, and the other is the Hostal de los Reyes Catolicos, which was built by King Ferdinand and Queen Isabella as a hospital for the poor and sick pilgrims who finally reached their destination. It is now a five-star hotel in the government's chain of paradors.

Even though it was a Monday in November there was standing room only for the noon mass. Neither George nor I could find a place to sit so we stood by one of the large columns. The archbishop read the mass and was assisted by eight other priests at the altar while two priests heard confessions along one of the walls. The confessionals were not enclosed. You knelt in front of the priest and looked him in the face while you said your confession.

During the mass the archbishop said that several pilgrims were in attendance. He began to read the names of the pilgrims, where they were from and where they began their journey.

"We have the following pilgrims who have walked from St. John Pied de Port, France, one pilgrim from America, one pilgrim from Brazil...," he said. I guess that was our two seconds of fame.

About five days ago Margaret discovered that in order to get the indulgence one had to also go to confession. That changed her whole outlook on the pilgrimage. Her enthusiasm quickly went downhill. She was not sure that she wanted to go to confession.

George had also been talking about this little technicality, which Margaret had referred to as the 'fine print' she had not noticed. As we stood there during the mass I noticed George looking, several times, at the priest who was hearing confessions. He finally decided to go, and went to stand in line. There was a woman confessing in front of him.

The main attraction of the special mass in this cathedral is the swinging of the largest incense dispenser in the world. It is called the *botafumeiro*. It is plated with silver and is about four feet high and probably three feet in circumference. It is suspended by one large rope from the center of the church, but there are also smaller ropes with a contraption made of pulleys which enable six men to put the *botafumeiro* in motion. As soon as it begins to move, the organ comes sharply alive with a tremendous sound. *Phantom of the Opera* was the first thought that crossed my mind. The organ music becomes louder and louder as the smoking *botafumeiro* swings higher and higher nearly touching the ceiling which is some ninety feet high. When the incense dispenser is at one of its highest positions you can see the fire inside. After about five minutes it is brought back to earth and stopped by the six men. At that point many people in the church clapped and then began to get up and leave. It was quite obvious what they had come to see.

Now that the crowd had thinned out I was finally able to get a seat. Jill then appeared and quietly sat down next to me.

"Hi, Jill," I whispered. "George is going to confession."

"I know," she said. "I couldn't believe it."

Actually George had not been able to talk to the priest yet. The woman in front of him was still making her confession. He finally made it, but communion had already been given so George would have to wait until tomorrow.

After the mass the three of us met up with Margaret and went to Casa Manolo for lunch. Margaret and Jill had eaten lunch there yesterday. Among tourists Casa Manolo was a well-known place to eat. The portions were huge and the price was cheap.

It was not too crowded today. One of the young men showed us to a table and gave us menus. For a small restaurant the menu is extensive.

After we had placed our orders, Margaret said, "The only thing wrong with this place is that they rush you."

"Now Margaret," I said, "I can remember when you were pestering waiters to hurry up and give us our bills."

"You don't have to worry about that here," she said. "They'll have your dessert and your bill on the table before you finish your main course."

"Well, I think I can understand why," I said. "They only have twelve tables and the prices are so low they probably have to have a lot of turnover."

The waiter did have our dessert on the table before we finished our main course. It wasn't necessary to select your dessert, they had only one, and it was rice pudding. They did not rush us today. Probably because it was not very crowded.

As we were eating, Margaret said, "George, I'm really proud of you. When was the last time you went to confession?"

"Eighteen years ago," he replied.

"Did the priest understand your Spanish?" Margaret asked.

"Not very well," George said, "but you know, it's the intent that's important."

"Now you know you're going to have to change all your evil ways," she said.

"Or, I guess I could always come back six years from now and walk again."

Jill said, "That woman in front of you was really taking a long time."

"I know," George agreed, "I thought she must have committed murder, or something really serious."

Finally I said, "Well, friends, if you will excuse me, I am going to leave you and do some souvenir shopping."

"We'll walk with you," Margaret said, "we're going back to the hotel for a while."

They left the restaurant with me and while we were walking back to our street we ran into Eva, Luis, and Augustino. Baltasar, who had been walking with them, did not live far from Santiago so they had gone home with him to stay overnight. They wanted to have a few more drinks with their old friends. George agreed to go with them, but Margaret, Jill and I declined.

There was a lively street here which had a number of bars. The bar at one end of the street was the Paris Bar and the one at the other end was the Dakar Bar. They told George they were going to take him from Paris to Dakar.

During the walk I had not spent nearly as much money as I had budgeted so I had plenty for souvenirs, actually too much, because weight was always a big problem. I knew that I was going to be loading up my backpack if I bought heavy things. I hit all the souvenir shops near the hotel, buying things which were not too heavy, and then waited around until George showed up later that evening.

While I was waiting I was sitting in a café across from our hotel writing in my journal when I saw four familiar pilgrims walking down the street. They were still carrying their backpacks. I went to the door and waved to them. We exchanged greetings. It was the two middle-aged Spanish couples. They had just gotten into town, and they were all walking together so I guess the warring couple had worked out their differences.

George and I would now have the last laugh. We'll teach Margaret to scoff at a couple of fast walkers like us!!

We had dinner again with Margaret and Jill. Things were not going too well for them. Margaret had lost the train schedule which she had gotten that morning so she and Jill had walked back to the station to get another one. The worst part was that Margaret bought tickets to Portugal. This caused a big argument to ensue. It wasn't the fact that she had bought tickets that was bad. The bad part was that she had bought tickets on a train which left at six o'clock in the morning when there was a train leaving at ten o'clock.

Jill said, "I can't understand why you did that. Getting there a few hours later wouldn't make any difference. You know I'm not a morning person. I just hate to get up early and if I do I'm crabby all day."

"That's for sure," said Margaret.

We were having a nice little snack that evening while this exchange was going on. It sounded much worse than it really was. By now they had gotten over the rough parts and they were pretty calm.

George and I walked Margaret and Jill back to their hotel and said good bye. We had enjoyed their company, and we would miss them. They always made things interesting.

That would be the last time we would see them.

SANTIAGO—NOVEMBER 23, 1999

▼

I got up at six-thirty and while I was getting ready, George woke up. Yesterday he had said he was going to walk to the train station with me.

"George, why don't you sleep in and rest your legs," I said. "You don't have to go to the station with me."

"Oh, no sir, Mister Bob," he said. "I'm going to walk with you."

The night before I had thrown out everything which I could afford to in order to pack in the souvenirs. The backpack was heavier than it had ever been. It was probably just a little over a mile to the train station so I wasn't too worried about it.

When George was ready we started off. It was still very early. The weather was cool and the sky was a little overcast. About half way to the station we found a café where we had our last breakfast together.

"Well, George," I said, "We have had a lot of coffees together, but I guess this will be the last one."

"Yeah, it has been a really great time for me," he said.

"What did you decide about your future?" I asked. "Did you make a decision about that?"

"I think that it's better that I break it off with Sayonara," he said. "If the job is still open, I will probably go to India. I think that would be best for her and for me."

I had never given George my opinion about his personal problem, but I did feel that he was doing the right thing.

I pulled on the heavy backpack and George and I continued on to the station. He walked in with me and we gave each other a big hug and said goodbye.

I figured that we had walked about 1,220,000 steps together. During that time I had grown to like this young man immensely. He was a gentleman. He was polite and he never had anything bad to say about anyone. He had a great sense of humor and every day he was good company. I sure would miss him.

While I was waiting in the station, I met Hans, another pilgrim, who was from Switzerland. I had seen him when we were walking into the city and, at that time, we just exchanged greetings. We talked for a minute and then went into the café for coffee.

While we were sipping our coffee he looked over at the counter and saw a stack of sandwiches. "Do you think we should buy some sandwiches to take on the train?" he asked.

"Oh, I don't think that will be necessary," I said with great confidence. "This should be a pretty big train and I'm sure they will have a dining car."

Hans did not speak English, so in his native language he said, "You speak good German."

Little did he know that in the fifteen minutes I had known him I had nearly exhausted my entire vocabulary.

Just a couple of minutes before nine o'clock an old train consisting of two cars, one first class and one second class, came into the station. Hans and I were both surprised to learn that this was our train. I thought, 'this is going to be a long ride to San Sebastian.'

As we found our seats in the first class car and the train began to move, Hans looked at me, laughed, and asked, "Which one do you think is the dining car?"

About eleven o'clock that morning I felt much better when they hooked up a dining car.

Just being able to sit in a comfortable seat and look out the window at the passing countryside was a real treat. Even though it was not as fast as the TGV, this train was a real luxury after walking all those days.

ABOUT THE AUTHOR

▼

Bob Tuggle retired from Harris Bank in Chicago after 38 years of service. He is a graduate of Northwestern University and has travelled to Europe, and Spain in particular, many times. He lives with his wife, Marie, in Darien, Illinois. Mr. Tuggle invites questions from anyone who is interested in walking the camino. He can be contacted by e-mail at BOB3701610@aol.com.